1000 Best
Quick and Easy
Organizing
Secrets

1000 Best Quick and Easy Organizing Secrets

Jamie Novak

SOURCEBOOKS, INC.®
NAPERVILLE, ILLINOIS

Published by Sourcebooks, Inc.
P.O. Box 4410, Naperville, Illinois 60567-4410
(630) 961-3900
FAX: (630) 961-2168
www.sourcebooks.com

Library of Congress Cataloging-in-Publication Data
Novak, Jamie.
  1000 best quick and easy organizing secrets / Jamie Novak.
     p. cm.
  Includes index.
  ISBN-13: 978-1-4022-0651-1
  ISBN-10: 1-4022-0651-8
  1. Storage in the home. 2. Orderliness. I. Title: One thousand best quick and easy organizing secrets. II. Title.

TX309.N68 2006
648'.8—dc22
                                                      2005031355

Printed and bound in Canada.
WC 10 9 8 7 6 5 4 3 2

Dedicated to

You! The person who wants to clear the clutter in your life so you can have more time to focus on the important things, because you realize this is not a dress rehearsal; it's the real thing.

And to Sue Novak who passed many of her organizing techniques down to me and taught me to treasure each moment I am given.

Contents

Acknowledgments

My sincere thanks to my editor at Sourcebooks, Bethany Brown. She made the entire process both easy and enjoyable. Her expertise was invaluable. Also much gratitude to the entire team at Sourcebooks. Those who with precision and patience brought my vision to the pages with skill and those who worked tirelessly behind the scenes to successfully launch the book. Also to my agent extraordinaire, Jessica Faust of BookEnds. Her belief in me from day one meant the world to me. I could never have imagined where we would end up after having met at NJRWA. To the professional organizers and experts who added wisdom to this book, namely, Don Aslett, America's #1 Cleaning Expert, Ramona Creel of Online Organizing, and Maria Gracia of Get Organized Now.

To my sisters who pitched in with enthusiasm every time I asked. You listened to me talk endlessly about the project for months, and you always smiled. For that I am deeply grateful. To everyone who in his or her own way unknowingly contributed to the book—you let me pick your brain about gardening, storing artwork, and using sticky notes. To those of you who receive my Clutter Challenge, are in my Clutter Clubs, and in the Master Mind Group, you posed great questions so I could be sure to include a solution. Your input was priceless—thank you.

And to you, my clients. Thank you for trusting me enough to share your lives with me. I stand in awe of all that you are able to accomplish with a little nudge and lots of laughter. I am fortunate to be able to do what I love each and every day, and I have you to thank for that. I am also indebted to each and every person who reads my books, attends my workshops, or watches my show. Thank you for allowing me to share my gift with you. We may not have had the chance to meet in person yet, but I sincerely hope we will, as you are very special to me.

Introduction

So, here's the deal. You have some areas you'd like to declutter, right? Well, I know how you can do it. Now, before you go thinking that this is just like every other organizing book for sale today I'll let you in on a little secret; my book is chock full of real ideas for real people. I promise not to suggest impractical solutions like adding a label to everything in your home or getting out of bed an hour earlier. That's just silly. You and I both know that given a choice between hopping out of bed and organizing a closet or staying asleep for one more hour, the alarm would be shut off in the blink of an eye.

1000 Best Quick and Easy Organizing Secrets contains all the best trade secrets and insider information from an expert professional organizer and is laid out in an easy-to-follow format. It's just like having me working with you in your home, only better. The book is less expensive, and you can work at your own pace.

You may be reading this and thinking, "This book is not meant for me, this stuff only works for people who are already somewhat organized or who possess some super organizing gene." Not true.

This book is for you! It is full of real tips for real people just like you whether you have items piled on every visible surface, closets bulging at the seams, or a car that never sees the inside of the garage. You may have been organized at one time or you may feel like you never quite got the hang of being organized. I'm here to tell you that you are not alone, and there is hope. The good news is organizing is not some astonishing ability. It is a completely learnable skill, just like tying your shoes or reciting the alphabet. You've probably learned to do both of those and you can learn to do this, too!

Laid out in an easy to read format the once confusing aspects of getting organized are broken down into sections. These no-fail tips will have you organized for life. You can do this, even if you've tried before and have met with resistance or failure. I'll show you all the steps, even the ones some organizers don't want you to know about. Inside I've covered topics left out by other books, such as what to do with clothes you've worn but are not ready to be laundered, CDs and DVDs in the car, email, photos and digital photos, staying organized while on vacation, and I've included very low or no cost solutions. I've also covered tips on maintaining your clutterproofed space—the most important and often most overlooked step in the whole organizing process.

Don't worry about finding the time to fit organizing into your already busy life, I've got that covered as well, with a whole chapter showing you how to find the time to get organized. Since getting organized "the Jamie Novak way" only requires eighteen minute blocks of time there will be no need for marathon sessions and no excuses since I know you can find eighteen minutes a week, without having to wake up any earlier.

You can live harmoniously in the present, by sorting out your past and planning for your future. You can spend your time on the important things in life. You should be making new memories, not trying to figure out how to store old ones.

As an organizer I know when you change the way you look at your stuff, your life changes. You start to value your time and money over belongings. And the benefits to getting organized are endless. You'll find yourself more connected with the people around you; you'll feel less stressed, more in control, and have more money. You will also gain a certain confidence; it feels good to know you can find what you need when you need it and that unexpected company can drop in unannounced without you feeling embarrassed. Clearing clutter helps you to reach your goals and you'll feel lighter with less stuff weighing you down.

Here's my promise to you: I will not try to reinvent you. Instead, we'll find what works for you and build on that. This is not about getting rid of all your stuff. It's about identifying what you use and love and then giving you access to it!

Momentum will build as you sort through your stuff. I guarantee, once you get started, it will not be as overwhelming as you may be imagining. Most people report that they anticipate it will be worse than it really is. In fact, many people actually enjoy the feeling of lightning up. Getting started is usually the hardest part. So, let's think of this as a treasure hunt and get excited about what you'll find instead of fearing what you'll come across. Don't waste another minute thinking about it, wondering about it, worrying about it; let's do something about it! Turn the page and together let's clear the clutter.

How to Use This Book

I wrote this book with you in mind. The busy, multitasking, over scheduled, "just saw it here a minute ago" clutter-prone person. I am not foolish enough to think that you have hours on end to lounge around eating bon bons while reading my book. I know you need straightforward, no fail information fast. Sound about right? Good, because if you're sitting on a couch eating bon bons for hours on end my guess is that you wouldn't need this book. Let me tell you how to get the most out of this book.

- If you are under a tight deadline to get a specific area under control, then take a moment to look over Part Six (page 81), which will give you the essentials in a nutshell. Then skip to the section for the area you want to clear and get to work. After you've tackled that area come back to the book and read how to maintain all your hard work, the most important part. This is the best way to approach decluttering for someone who has guests coming in a few days, who has a contractor coming to look at a space for a remodeling project or who is under some other type of deadline.

- If you feel overwhelmed and are not sure where to start then ease into the whole process by beginning with Part One: Setting Up for Success page 9. Once you are all set up continue reading to learn how to fit time in your week to get organized. After that, keep reading. Each subsequent part will offer you valuable ideas and motivation. Before you realize it, you will be prompted to take a small step. Once you do that you are home free! You are just a few more small steps away from success. This is the best way for someone who has had false starts before.

- If you have an endless number of hours and nothing to do with them then read the book cover to cover. Highlight all the times I use the word 'the' and then email me. Someone who has that sort of time and can be that detail oriented should probably be working for me! I'm kidding, but I do want to be clear that you don't have to have a ton of free time for this book to work for you.

I do not want this book to become another statistic, cast into a pile of books you're going to read "one day," sitting on your nightstand hoping that you will have enough time before your eyes close as your head hits the pillow to dig out the book and crack it open. Instead, I want you to keep this book near you at all times. Even if you only have a moment, reading just one tip will put you one step closer to success. So promise me that the book will not end up shoved under something or in a drawer somewhere. Keep it out and reach for it daily. The key to success is tiny, consistent movements toward the goal.

Part One:

Setting Up for Success

So let's just say it, you own lots of stuff. Your stuff may be bulging out of closets, sliding off tabletops or piled higher than a small child. Sure, you may not be able to sit down at the table without relocating piles and you may have to park in the driveway because the garage is full of stuff. Let me assure you of two things. One, you are not alone, and two, it's all right. All the answers you need are right here in this book.

For some strange reason, many people who own lots of stuff tend to think of it as a character flaw. Have you ever felt like there was something fundamentally wrong with you? A sense of hopelessness may have washed over you as you watched one of those "oh this is so easy, anyone can do it" organizing shows. Or you may have read yet another article on organizing while standing in line at the grocery store, thinking,

"Hey I can do that!" and you took a whole weekend, pulled everything out of a space and put it back perfectly. Now let me guess how long it stayed that way, about one week? If you have little children or a spouse, it was probably less time, right?

And then as if you didn't already feel bad enough, your perfectly organized friend pops by unannounced. You know the one, she's always ahead of schedule, has a pen and paper on hand, and there is not one outdated magazine in her home. And when you feel compelled to meet her on the porch because inviting her in would embarrass you, the guilt really gets going. You feel even less successful and less worthy. Sometimes those feelings translate into you buying even more stuff! See the pattern?

People may have said mean things or even called you a pack rat or messy. They may have even said that they could clear out your stuff in one day, by simply throwing it all in a dumpster. Remember, when they say things like that they have no idea the attachment you may have to your belongings. They may be speaking out of frustration, and truthfully, you may have thought those same things some days.

You may be surrounded by a lifelong accumulation of stuff. Or it may have happened more recently, with a major change in your life such as a move, birth of a child, death of a loved one, or a physical or mental challenge. Consider it an obstacle; if you once were more organized then you are today do not strive to return to your more organized roots, you are a different person today.

Instead of trying to work backwards simply decide to be a new more organized you.

Plans are important and you need one. Imagine setting off on a cross-country road trip with no map. What do you think the chances are you would reach your destination? Slim to none, right? Same thing with getting organized, you need a map to follow. Having a plan to follow will allow you to be sure you have what you need before you start, organize your thoughts so you can focus on the organizing, and check off as you go along so you feel a sense of accomplishment and feel confident that you are on the right path. I want you to be successful; you want to be successful so let's create a plan for success right now!

1.

Making the Plan

1. Accept what is. It's difficult not to feel over-whelmed by all the stuff that has collected around your home. You might not like being at home much and look for reasons to spend your days outside your house. Or you might berate yourself each time you look at the clutter asking yourself, "How did I let it get like this?" Give yourself permission to accept what is, knowing that you are now creating a plan to conquer the clutter for good. Spend your time and energy doing something about it instead of feeling bad about how it is.

2. Every organizer has a bag of tricks, commonly stored in a tool chest. You'll want to make your own clutter-conquering tool chest, so that you will have what you need when you need it. This will save a ton of time. Instead of starting a project and having to put it on hold as you go in search of a marker or plastic bag, you'll have one at your fingertips. Your bag of tricks should include a large tote bag, a plastic bin with handles (laundry baskets work well), and the following items: Ziploc bags (small & large), trash bags, tape measure, timer, label maker and extra labels, notebook, pen, shredder, sticky notes, permanent marker, stack of laundry baskets for sorting, empty boxes, and a list of local charities you might want to call on.

3. If you are missing any item(s) do not wait until you find them or buy them to get started. Simply make a note of what you need to add to the tool chest and continue. That's it. Your tool chest is ready to go, and you are ready for action!

4. A house tour is the first thing I want you to do, it's how you'll be able to see with a fresh eye all the hot spots where clutter piles up. The result will be a master list of areas you want to tackle. You'll only need about thirty minutes and your notebook. Start at the door you use to come in the home most often, open the door and pretend you are welcoming in someone who you have always admired and hoped to meet one day. Now show them around your home and as you give the tour, note in your notebook all the areas that make you cringe. Do not edit your list; note everything even if you have no idea if it can be fixed, how it could be done, or what it would cost. If you have thirty minutes, conduct your own home tour now.

5. Create a master plan by compiling the notes from your home tour. Take a few minutes to make one master list of all the areas you want to work on. Your list may include such items as papers off the counter, toys off the floor, weed magazines, thin out closet, clean out bathroom vanity drawers, and so on. This list is your master list of short and long-term goals.

BONUS TIP:
You might choose to focus on a "room of the month." By working on one room at a time you'll be sure to meet your deadline within a year.

6. Take your own before and after photos to see how far you've come. They also act as a reminder of the way you don't want things to go back to.

7. To be successful it is important to narrow your focus so you are not dispersing your energy and doing just a little in many spots. From your master list, pick your top three hot spots. Working on one hot spot until it is clutter-free and then moving on is the only way to success. You'll want to select the ones that have the biggest impact on your day-to-day living. For example, if you argue with your partner over toys on the floor, that might make the short list. If you are paying late fees because mail is left unopened for weeks, then that may make your short list. Or if you waste time each day looking for something to wear, your closet might make the list. Create your list now.

8. Put a temporary freeze on shopping. Agree not to buy anything, not even containers to help you get organized. At this point you are not exactly sure what you have or where you are going to store it. Buying more things at this point will only add to the amount of things you own and have to sort through. Instead, save your money since you'd likely find out that what you bought today wouldn't work anyway.

9. No more garage sales or hand me downs until you organize what you already own. And if you have one of the bumper stickers that reads "This car stops at garage sales," take it off!

10. If you find it difficult to stop buying items, then consider collecting pictures of the items you want to buy. Place the pictures in a file folder and decide whether to buy the items a little later on.

11. Attack visible clutter first. We like instant gratification, even when clearing clutter we like to see results immediately. What better way then to deal with visible clutter first. When you clear the stuff in your way that gets the ball rolling to tackle the unseen places such as attics and basements.

12. Set a deadline. There is a rule that says a project will expand to fill the amount of time allotted. By setting a deadline for when you will have each stage of your decluttering project complete, you have a much better chance of being successful. Keep two things in mind: make your goal realistic, and break up large goals into smaller intermediate goals.

13. When you know why you want to do something it makes it easier to get through the tough times. So take a moment, jot down the top three reasons why you want to get organized and keep them in mind as you take the steps to reach your goal.

14. It's funny, but most of us tend to get more done when we know someone is going to check up on us. Find yourself a trusted friend or family member and ask them to keep track of your progress. This can be a huge motivator. In fact, it works even better if the two of you are both in decluttering mode, you can become clutter buddies and support each other!

15. Take breaks and do not do marathon sessions. Remember that slow and steady wins the race. Plan to work in small blocks of time, with plenty of reenergizing breaks in between.

16. List a bunch of rewards you might like to indulge in. After a job well done pick one and enjoy some well-deserved time off. Rewards can be anything you want them to be—reading a novel, getting a manicure, watching a movie, having coffee with a friend, going on a date with your spouse, or taking a nap—whatever works for you, aside from buying something.

CLUTTER-CLEARING PLEDGE

Sign this clutter-clearing pledge and reread it often. It will make the process more official and help you get through any rough patches.

I _____ promise to make every effort to break old habits and patterns that no longer serve me so that I can be more organized. I pledge to leave every space better than I found it. I will stop putting myself down. Instead of focusing on how things got this way, I will work to change them. I promise to forgive myself for past purchases that were not right for me and I will make better selections in the future. I will make a clutter-free home a priority and do at least one thing a day to reach that goal. I will not rush myself, but I will stay on track to meet my realistic timeline, keeping in mind that the clutter did not happen in twenty-four hours and will not be fixed overnight. I will allow for potential setbacks and view them as learning experiences, not failures. I will start again. I will remember that each person is an individual, and I will stop comparing myself to others around me. I will give up my unrealistic expectation of myself and dreams of perfection. Instead, I will focus on progress. I will do my best to maintain my decluttered space. I promise that I will seek the support and solutions that I need, understanding that organizing is a skill to be learned not a mysterious talent or something I was born without. When I feel like giving up I will remember why I want to have a clutter-free space. I will look at the room as if it is already how I want it, so I can inspire myself to continue. Finally, at the end of each day I promise to take note of what I accomplished and pat myself on the back instead of focusing on what is still left to do.

Signing this pledge today affirms that I believe in myself and know that I can bring about a significant change, starting now!

The top three reasons why I want to get organized:

1. _____
2. _____
3. _____

Signed: _____
Dated: _____

2.

Using Your Organizing Style to Your Advantage

17. The true test of whether a space is organized is not how it looks but how it functions. Can you find what you need when you need it? (The standard would be a minute or less.) If you can, then it's organized, if not, recheck the system because it needs a tune up.

18. Is your organizing style an A, B, or C? Do you prefer things Available (the "leave it out so I don't forget it" mentality)? Are you a Basket kind of person who likes items out but contained? Or a Cabinet kind of person, preferring items out of sight and behind closed doors? The great thing is that we do not have to reinvent you; we simply need to discover your way of doing things so we can duplicate what works and stop doing what is not working.

19. There is nothing wrong with you if you struggle with clutter. In fact, since you are reading this book you should feel proud that you are taking steps to learn the skill of how to be organized.

FAST

Get started fast by taking a moment to define your organizing style, are you an A, a B, or a C. Knowing this will help you organize in a way that is easy for you to maintain.

Part Two:

Understanding Clutter

Into every life some stuff must fall. But does that mean we have to hold onto it? The answer is a resounding no. So why do we? Let me count the ways: it's still good; it was free; I'll get to it later; it reminds me of something; it might come in handy one day; it was a gift; I'll be that size again; in case we have another baby...The list goes on and on, and I've heard them all. You can't give me a new-fangled reason. This chapter is going to challenge the validity of your excuses.

A few of these suggestions may make you feel a little uncomfortable, and that's all right. I simply want to get you thinking. I am not going to force you to part with things that you are not ready to let go of. But my guess is that some of what I've written you already know. Some of it may even make you smile.

Keep in mind that when your relationship with stuff changes, your life changes. You begin to uncover your life; it's waiting for you under all the stuff. To see how much time you'll have back in your day add up all the time you spend looking for misplaced items with the time you spend worrying about organizing all your stuff. That time could be used doing things! Learn how to deal with the emotions, habits, and patterns that have prevented the clutter from being dealt with once and for all. Because as we all know, we are each given twenty-four hours a day and we don't know how many more days we have left. So if you have been waiting to invite people over to entertain, or if you have been putting off starting a new hobby or taking a class, today is the day. I am sorry to disappoint you, but there will *never* be a time when everything is taken care of. As you clear up the stuff from today, more stuff is coming for you to deal with tomorrow. Balance is the key. Do some work, but don't forget to play, because this is your life not a dress rehearsal. So what have you been wanting to change? And when are you going to change it?

Remember this is not about just getting rid of things; it's about identifying what's important to you and giving you easy access to it.

3.

What Is Clutter?

20. Any item that does not have a designated place to be put away when not in use is considered homeless. Anything without a home is considered clutter. Think of the new set of glasses you purchased on sale that have been sitting on the counter while you try to figure out where to put them.

21. Love it or lose it. Only have things in your home that you use and love. If it is not something you need or that brings you joy then it qualifies as clutter. Think of the picture frame you were given as a gift that is just not your style. You'll never display it, but still you keep it.

22. Any item relating to an incomplete task is definitely clutter. Think of the cross-stitch kit you tucked in a drawer when you intended to learn how to cross stitch. Now, you have no interest, but you still have the kit. That's clutter.

23. Items in need of repair are clutter. Think of that pile of mending in the laundry room, which includes the newborn outfit in need of a seam for a child who is now two. Make a new house rule: In our home, any item in need of repair is fixed within twenty-four hours, or we let it go.

24. Holding onto items for the future, without a specific date or purpose in mind is called a dream. You might plan to sell your stuff at a garage sale, but without a definite date on the calendar, these items are clutter. Have a plan for the items or let them go.

25. We've all experienced the challenge of overflowing stuff—the drawer that cannot shut unless you push things down or the closet that you need to wear a hardhat to open because items tend to come crashing down. These are both examples of too many things in a small space.

26. When you have a bunch of mixed categories together, it makes items difficult to find and clutter becomes out of control.

27. Often, clutter is simply a postponed decision. Whenever you put off making a decision about something, you tend to leave it out until you get back to it. All those things sitting out waiting to be decided on in the meantime are clutter.

FAST

Get started fast: pick one of the definitions of clutter and make a choice now not to fall victim to it.

4.

Reasons Why We Keep Clutter

28. "It'll come in handy one day." Holding onto an item just in case sometime in the future you might need it creates clutter now and forces you to try to remember you have it in case you need it one day. On the other hand, if you passed it along someone who needs it today can start to use it.

29. "I'll get to it later." That's one phrase that can bring to a screeching halt any advancement in clutter-clearing. You innocently lay a coat over the chair because you plan to use it later, or you place the pile of mail on the table to go through later. But later may not come. Plans change. Try to adopt a do it now mentality.

30. "It's still good." You need to recognize that things are usually built to last. This means that the margarine container, the plastic shopping bags, and the crib your child outgrew may all still be good. But are they still good to you? Unless the things you are holding on to are useful to you, you should get rid of them.

31. "But I might need it." The fact that one day you might need it doesn't mean you need to be the one to store it. If you haven't used it awhile (you pick the time frame—six months, one season, a year) then let it go. Someone needs it right now and could use it. If giving it away is not an option then try finding someone who can "borrow" it; if you need the item later you can "borrow" it back.

32. "I love it." Often while clearing out areas you'll come across items you'd forgotten about and when you see them again you exclaim, "I love this." I encourage you to really think about that statement. If you'd forgotten you even owned it how much could you have really enjoyed it. And if you didn't take the time to care for it properly and give it the attention it deserves then maybe it is time to pass it along to someone who has the time and desire to give it proper attention.

33. "I'm in the middle of organizing." Not leaving time to clean up after you have been sorting and organizing is a major blunder. The space will look worse than when you started, plus all your hard work will go down the tubes when your piles of items are mixed back together.

34. "I do everything in here." One of the best things to do when you are getting organized is to step back and figure out how you want your space to function. Once you know that, you can plan to organize the space to meet the needs. If your spare bedroom now functions as a junk room, you can plan to set it up as a craft room or guest room and let this guide your efforts.

35. "I don't know where to begin." The most effective way to work on multiple areas is to choose one to work on first. Then see it through start to finish. Splitting your focus and working on multiple areas simultaneously will only slow you down and since you will not see significant change in any one area it is difficult to feel successful.

36. "There's too much to do." If you are unsure what to do to get started or feel stuck in a rut simply take a very small step towards something to break the blockade. Focus on progress not perfection.

37. "I can't do it by myself." Having a clutter buddy will be important to help you get over any rough patches as you get organized. A non-judgmental friend or family member is often a good choice. They can talk you through rationalizing if you really need and use things you want to hold onto. If you feel you need more structured assistance you can opt to hire a professional organizer, work with a therapist, or locate a clutter support group.

38. "I'm a natural procrastinator." One way to deal with putting things off is to give yourself a reward for a job well done. For example, if you have been meaning to watch a movie, then put it on only after you have organized the area you have been promising yourself you would get to. Another option is to do the hardest task first. For example if you have a list of three tasks, do the one on the list you dread the most and once it is done the other tasks will be a piece of cake. Another solution is to tell someone you are going to do it. They will then be able to hold you accountable and since you'll want to report a success, you'll be more likely to actually do it.

39. "I'm such a mess." Stop labeling yourself as disorganized. Instead, think of the process as a treasure hunt to uncover the organized person inside.

40. "She who dies with the most shoes wins." False. More is not usually better. Instead, choose the items you love and have them around you.

41. "I'll just put this all over here." No more scoop and dump. No matter what do not allow yourself to scoop up a bunch of stuff, especially papers, and toss them somewhere. Even if company is on your doorstep you cannot do the scoop and dump. Try this new house rule: In our home, we do not stash piles. We spend a few minutes sorting through them and putting the stuff away, even if company is on the doorstep.

42. "This brings back memories." Live in the present. It is very common to hold onto things from your past if you have fond memories of years gone by. Maybe the items remind you of when your children were young or when you lived in a certain home. Allow yourself to store the memories so there is more room to live in the present.

43. One more word about memories: mementos, souvenirs, and handcrafted projects may hold a special meaning for you. The T-shirt you wore on your honeymoon, the snow globe from your last vacation, the picture your child drew, the dress you wore to your sister's wedding, the list can go on and on. Don't panic; these are not items you'll need to part with. You simply need to store them so that they are safe and you can look through them from time to time reliving the memory.

44. "One day I'll…"Alternatively, you may be living for the future. You may have grand plans of how you will spend your time when you have more of it. So you hold onto all sorts of items thinking, "One day I'll…" Instead of keeping the stuff let someone else use it now. Keep a running list of the items. so when you make the time to do the projects you can get the stuff you need.

45. "If I do all this, what'll be next?" Highly efficient people are usually expected to do more. Could that thought possibly be causing you to not want to be organized? You might be afraid of what will be expected of you when you are able to use your time more effectively.

46. "It has to be perfect." Step back for a moment and look at what your expectations are. Perfect is a high standard to set. With such an expectation, it will be challenging to do anything that measures up. Consider resolving to do it well, then in your spare time you can choose to go back and perfect it. Focus on progress not perfection.

47. "It's even worse than it used to be." Agree to maintain. Not maintaining a space once it is decluttered is often the reason why an area slides back to how it used to be, or worse.

48. "Two steps forward, one step back." Allow for setbacks. Keep in mind that you are creating new organized habits, so if you slide back a little into old clutter causing habits and patterns simply recognize it and begin again.

49. "How did things get this way?" Sometimes figuring out where you picked up your clutter causing habits is the missing piece to the puzzle that will help you break the habit. Figure out where you learned your habits and what makes you continue the pattern.

50. "As soon as I saw it, I knew I had to have it." Think before you buy. Ask yourself "where will I put this?" before you buy an item. If you have a good answer then buy it, if not then wait to make the purchase until a later date. Bringing anything new into your home that you do not have a home for will just mean you have more stuff to organize. Also avoid stopping by garage sales or accepting hand-me-downs. Try shopping from a list.

51. "This will be great to put things in." Stop buying containers and asking yourself what you can store inside it. Instead, measure the item you have to store and buy a container specifically for it.

52. "It was on sale." Stocking up on something because it is a bargain or purchasing misfit clothing because you "could probably wear this some day" are not deals by any stretch of the imagination. Unless you really go through twelve tubes of toothpaste or want to make it your life's mission to find a shirt to match the inexpensive pair of paisley capri pants from your favorite designer, practice passing up so called sales.

53. "It was free." It could be a pen from your doctor's office or a mug from the bank. Unless you need another pen or mug, these items take up your space forcing you to clean around them while you are providing free advertising!

54. "I paid good money." No matter what you paid for it, if you keep it, but don't use it, it is still a waste. Resolve yourself to the fact that you did not make the best purchase decision and let the item go to someone who will love and use it.

55. "I'm saving it for my garage sale." If you are holding onto things with plans to make a large profit at a garage sale you might want to think twice. With the time and effort involved, garage sales are not all that easy. If you enjoy hosting garage sales then mark the next one on your calendar so the season does not pass you by and go for it. If this is not your favorite way to spend your time then consider donating the items for a tax receipt and take the deduction.

56. "I'll sell it on eBay." Online auctions and consignment shops are similar traps that can spell disaster. The items can take up a tremendous amount of space for a long amount of time and not sell for enough to make the trouble worth it.

57. "It's a collectible." If you find yourself holding onto collections of things, teapots, comic books, dolls, and so on then consider this; it is costing you money to store these items. You can easily figure out how much by taking your mortgage or rent payment and dividing it by the estimated square footage of your home. Then you'll know how much you pay per square foot, which means if you are storing a box of old toys and it is three square feet, then you are paying $30 a month to hold onto the past.

58. "Someday it'll be worth something." It's only worth something if you can find someone willing to pay for it. Instead of allowing the item to take up valuable space in your home pass it along. If it makes you feel better, log onto an online auction site to see what your item is selling for. Chances are the value is perceived and not actual, and you'll feel better about letting it go.

59. "It's so cute." Cute often means nonfunctional. Try to stay away from cute things and opt instead for things that are more functional. A porcelain figurine can be cute; a decorative mug to hold pens is functional.

60. "I'm afraid of not having enough." Sometimes what we learned growing up sticks with us as adults. One example is the fear of not having enough because of a time when there was not enough like during the depression. If you were taught to be thrifty and reuse or hold onto things out of fear, then you may be repeating those habits today.

61. "It was a gift." At some point, we are all given a not so great gift, but the thought still counts. After you say thank you for the thoughtful gift it is your choice what to do with it from then on. You can opt to pass it along to someone who will use and love it. The key is to remember that the giver would prefer that you pass the gift along then be burdened with it.

FAST
Get started fast by looking over the list and figure out three of the biggest reasons why you hold onto clutter. Then determine what steps you are going to take to help you overcome your clutter-prone ways.

Part Three:

Getting Motivated

If I were to ask you why you want to get organized, what would you say? Your answer would probably have something to do with how you will feel when the clutter is gone. For example, you might feel more in control, more successful, or you might feel like you could finally start to reach your other goals, ones that have probably taken a back seat for too long. Everyone has their own reasons as to why they want to get organized—what are yours?

Figuring out your motivation to simplify makes it easier to keep going even if the going gets tough. Something drew you to this book at this point in your life. What was it? Did you have yet another disagreement with your partner over clutter? Did you have to pay a service fee this month because the bills went out late again? Do you fall into bed every night dead tired but not able to recount exactly what you did all day although you know you were busy? Are you just plain fed up?

Whatever your motivation take note of it, step back for a moment, and imagine what it would be like to have the clutter gone. Would you be able to climb into bed with out moving laundry? Would your bills be paid on time? Would you eat together as a family more often since you'd be able to see the table? Would you feel more in control or entertain more? Knowing what clutter costs you and picturing the end result of decluttering is one of the best ways to get inspired to do something about it.

5.

What Is Clutter Costing You?

62. Having lots of stuff can create daily frustrations. Would you like more free time in your day or do you choose to surround yourself with stuff which sucks up your valuable time as you sort it, care for it, clean around it, look for it, and worry about it? This moment is all you have. Simplify and get back all that you've lost.

63. Missed opportunities can cost you close connections with friends and family. Coming across an invitation after the date of the event might mean you missed an important family or good friend's party.

64. Feeling overwhelmed, stressed, frazzled, and out of control can cause you to be short-tempered, impatient, and aggravated. Stress can even take a toll on your health. No belonging is worth paying that price.

65. Disharmony in a relationship is another consequence of clutter. If you and your partner have differing clutter styles than you may find clutter a common source for disagreements.

66. If you have little ones in your home, you know they learn by example. If they see you leaving a mess in your wake, they will be apt to do the same. Just the opposite is also true, you can instill non-clutter causing habits in them.

67. Clutter can zap your energy faster than any aerobics class. Laying eyes on piles of unsorted papers can turn a good mood sour in a second.

68. Clutter has a funny way of keeping us stuck. You surround yourself with mementos of the past and things you plan to do in the future which keeps you focused on what was or what might have been and prevents you from living in the present.

69. Clutter can make you feel confused. You may start to wonder if something is wrong with your memory because you're more apt to lose or forget things.

70. If you prefer to have people call before they drop by or you opt to hold events outside your home because you're embarrassed about the mess, then clutter is affecting your ability to connect with the people you love and enjoy spending time with.

71. If you feel uncomfortable scheduling a repairman to come fix the dryer or a contractor to give you an estimate on a remodeling project then clutter is stopping you from taking care of necessities and may cause you to put your dreams on hold.

72. Your ability to be creative is lost when you are surrounded by too much stuff. Being organized does not squash creativity, in fact the reverse is true. Your creativity is fueled in an environment where ideas can be captured and acted upon.

73. Knowing what you own and being able to display treasures allows you to enjoy your possessions instead of having them lost and hidden under and behind other things.

74.

Piles of clutter and lots of stuff make housecleaning more of a chore. Cleaning around and under things is time-consuming and difficult.

6.

Clearing Clutter All the Way to the Bank

75. When bills go unopened or are sent late the excess charges add up quickly. Staying on top of your financial commitments will save you a whole lot of money.

76. Most companies that offer rebates bank on the fact that you will forget to mail it in with all its proper pieces. Don't let your money go unclaimed. Even a $10 rebate is ten more dollars in your pocket.

77. When you do not plan ahead, rush charges can eat up lots of your money. If you wait until the last day before ordering a gift you may end up spending a great deal extra on special delivery. If you wait to the last minute to mail holiday packages and opt to send them overnight so they reach the recipient in time, the fees can really add up.

78. By not staying on top of routine matters, like doctor and dentist appointments, regular car maintenance, and trips to the veterinarian you may find you need emergency care that can be time-consuming and costly. It is much less expensive to drive your car in for regular oil changes than it is to pay for a new engine because the old one has seized.

79. Buying a duplicate of something you already have at home but cannot find wastes a lot of money. In addition, it takes up extra space you could be using to store something you really need.

BONUS TIP:
To reduce the chance of rebuying an item, take all your purchases out of the bag as soon as you walk in the door with them.

80. You may buy more than what you really need of something because you are not sure how much of it you already have at home. You've spent money that you didn't have to and also have to find a place to put all the extra stuff you bought.

81. If you buy something for future use but do not remember you have it to use when you need it, it wastes money. Unworn clothing with tags still on, purchases still in plastic bags, and items bought on sale with no direct purpose in mind are examples of money not well spent.

82. Many job performance evaluations rate you on your level of organization. Coworkers and superiors alike notice a messy desk, missed deadlines, and delayed projects due to lost items. Raises and promotions are most definitely affected by clutter.

83. Renting a storage facility is one of the biggest money wasters of all. If you are storing things off site because you do not have enough room where you live then you need to downsize immediately. The only exception would be if you are moving in the next month or two and have items in transition. Even then, look carefully at what you are paying to store. You can probably rebuy it later, if you need it, for less than you would spend to store it.

84. It is extremely common to find some amount of money while getting organized. A stash of coins, forgotten un-cashed checks, cash in a greeting card, and unused gift certificates are some of the ways it can pay to declutter.

85. Another way to profit from decluttering is to hold a yard sale, take items to a consignment shop, or give items to a local auction to be auctioned off on your behalf. Money from the sale goes into your pocket.

86. Another way to benefit from decluttering while helping others is to pass your items onto charities. This allows you to take tax deductions for the donations.

FAST
Get started fast by choosing three reasons why you want to clear the clutter. Write them on a piece of paper and post them where you can see them. Review them every day to help you maintain the momentum.

Part Four:

Dealing with Mental Clutter

You know that nagging feeling that you forgot something? Annoying, isn't it? Even more annoying is the list that pops up in your mind as you are trying to fall asleep. You know the one. It goes like this, you have to call and change the dentist appointment, you were supposed to drop something off to a friends house, you are in charge of the bake sale, the bills are due, the kitchen faucet is leaking, and so on.

With all we have to remember, it's no wonder we misplace our keys and glasses. Let's face it; we can only remember so much at one time. If you think of your mind as a drinking glass, imagine pouring water into that glass. Each drop of water is something you need to remember. Soon the glass will fill to the top and eventually begin to overflow. The same thing is true for our mind, when we try to remember everything in our heads, it is inevitable that something "leaks" out.

Mental clutter can be as difficult to deal with or even worse than physical clutter. It can make us feel distracted and out of focus. In this section, I've listed all the best ways to clear the mental clutter.

7.

Mind Clearing Techniques

87. Brain dump. This is the best way to release all those "to do" thoughts from your mind. Grab a spiral bound notebook (so the pages do not fall out) and start writing. Write everything that comes to mind in any order it comes. Do not edit yourself, simply write. At the end you are going to be left with a page or pages of action items. Now you can very easily list like tasks with like: things you need to buy, calls you need to make, things you need to do. Once you have these smaller lists, you can start to take action with the comfort of knowing all the items are on pages in your own notebook for easy reference. Plus, your mind will be clear, allowing you to focus on just a few things at a time, a less stressful way of living.

88. Give your notebook a home. In order for you to continue writing in your notebook, you need to feel confident that the notebook will always be on hand. Choose one spot now as the home for your notebook; it may be a drawer, a hook, your tote bag, your purse, wherever. Carry it with you when you go out and always be sure to return it there when you are finished using it.

89. To keep the mental clutter at bay you will need to adopt a new habit of writing everything down in the notebook and only in the notebook. This means no more Post-it notes, scraps of paper, or jotting things down on the backs of envelopes.

90. Keep it simple. If you have two or more subjects that you feel deserve their own notebook space, consider working from the front for one subject and turning the notebook over and working from the back for the other. Alternatively, you can choose a notebook with subject tabs and use one subject area per topic.

91.

You may find it is more helpful to write some information directly on your calendar. For example, the date of an upcoming surprise birthday party will do you little good in the notebook. This event needs to be noted on the calendar. However, the gift you want to purchase and the directions are good things to write in the notebook. That way while at the store, you will have the list of gifts to buy. Additionally, while driving to the party, you will have the directions which you jotted in your notebook which you carry with you.

FAST
Get started fast by locating a notebook you can use and start it off with a brain dump.

Part Five:

Making the Most of Your Time

Remember as a child how it felt like it took forever for your birthday or the holidays to roll around? So, how is it that today as soon as one event passes, it feels like it is time to start preparing for the next big item on your "to do" list? And speaking of "to do" lists, are you making one? Writing a plan for your day is one of the best ways to maximize the time you have. But do not over book yourself—a common mistake most of us make. Your daily list of things to do should be comprised of the top five to seven tasks that need your attention. That way, at the end of the day, each item will be crossed off and you can throw the list away. A good rule of thumb to know you have too much on your plate is to list what you have to do. If you use the word "then" five times or more chances are you are overbooked. An example is: Today I am going to put in a load of laundry, then I'm going grocery shopping, then I'm calling my insurance company, then I'm picking up the kids from school, then I'm stopping to grab the dry cleaning, then I'm making dinner, then I'm going to a scrapbooking class, then I'm cooking brownies for the bake sale, then I'm packing lunches, and then I'm going to bed. A list such as this is unrealistic and does not allow you to enjoy any one of those tasks since you'll be rushing from place to place and crossing your fingers that you do not hit a red light or get stuck behind a slow driver.

Part of making a plan to conquer clutter includes finding the time to schedule clutter dates. If you feel overwhelmed, short on time, or frantic, or if you are always running behind, showing up late, and forgetting things, then you need more time. The average American spends fifty-five minutes a day looking for lost or misplaced items. Imagine getting back even a fraction of that time! Here are some of the very best ways to discover lost time and to make the most of the time you do have.

8.

Tips for Time Balance

92. For one whole week, pay attention to how you spend your time. You might be surprised to find there are small changes you can make which will give you back pockets of time. For example, would using a letter opener speed up the process of opening the mail?

BONUS TIP:
You can use those pockets of time to complete quick tasks such as weeding a Rolodex or checking to be sure all the pens in your pen cup work. Or you can work for just a few minutes on a large task to at least get it started. The best way to remember about these tasks is to write a master list of projects, and next to the task write a guesstimate of the amount of time it will take. Then post the list on the inside of a kitchen cabinet door and the next time you have just a few minutes, instead of wasting it away, check your list and do something.

93. Not wearing shoes (at least not ones that have been outside) in the house cuts down housecleaning time significantly, studies say 87 percent of the dirt in the home comes into your home on the bottom of your shoes.

94. Store items where you need them in order to stop wasting time by running up and down stairs for things as small as a pair of scissors. This may mean duplicating some things, like a stick vac, cleaning supplies, scissors, and telephones on each level, but imagine the time you'll get back when you can answer the phone without having to run down a flight of stairs to locate it. This rule can be applied all over; for example, keep a pair of sunglasses in each car or one in your purse and one in your tote bag.

95. If you find yourself running around in the morning in a mad rush to get ready, consider saving time by preparing the night before. You can select your outfit, charge your cell phone, fill the coffee maker, and pack your lunch.

INSIDER TIP:
Create an exit center where you can place all the items you'll need for the day, a slim table near the entryway works well.

96. Even adults can become tired with the same old routine. Consider swapping chores with your spouse on a monthly basis or whenever you become bored. This is also a great way to learn new skills.

97. Your friends and family need to grocery shop too. Try running errands together so that you can socialize as you tick tasks off your "to do" list.

98. Hang a tote bag on the handle of the door you use most often. In it place the items you need to take with you: bills to mail, videos to return, library books to give back, directions to the place you are driving, play tickets, and so on. Then as you leave grab the tote and you'll have everything you need. Ensure success of this new plan by always bringing the tote back into the house and hanging it up so it can be filled for the next day.

BONUS TIP:
As soon as you come home from shopping take all of your purchases out of their bags. This will help remind you to put things away, so that you can find them when you need them.

99. Instead of going to two stores, swap errands with a friend or neighbor who has to go to the same places. If you need to go to the post office take a package for your neighbor, then he or she can pick up your dry cleaning when they go to get theirs.

100. Children love to help. Consider asking them to load the dryer, vacuum, dust, and so on. Many kids love to skate around on the hardwood floors with dust clothes on their feet, exercising and cleaning in one.

101. Create new house rules. Once the routine is established you can decide where to draw the line. Your new rules might include something like "If dirty laundry is not in the designated space by wash day it will not get done until the next wash day."

102. Mounds of laundry can accumulate seemingly overnight, so get everyone to pitch in. Request that dirty clothing be brought to a designated area on certain days. You can even ask that it be placed in one of three piles: whites, darks, or colors. Then you can do the wash and put it away or leave it ready to be picked up and taken to its home. Having a routine of when the wash gets done will stop you from feeling like you are always doing laundry.

103. Turning on the washing machine at night before bed saves time, in the morning you can simply pop the clothes in the dryer.

104. Many little tasks and chores have to be done in a home, from replacing a light bulb to fixing a squeaky door. Individually they may seem like they take small amounts of time. But when a few tasks pile up it takes a lot of time. Try planning one night or weekend day a month to deal with these tasks. By designating one specific time, you'll have the tools out and complete a few tasks at the same time, plus it won't feel like you're constantly doing a repair or reminding a partner about a repair every week.

105. Make it a plan that when you adjust your clocks for daylight savings time, you do other chores like replacing water and air filters, tossing expired medications and vitamins, checking the batteries in your smoke and carbon monoxide detectors, and making sure all the light bulbs on the car work. Make this task easier by writing the item numbers of the filters and replacement parts and posting them on the inside of the pantry door in the kitchen.

106. A simple way to remind your partner about the tasks they are responsible for is to post the "honey-do" list on the bathroom mirror. They can't help but look at it.

107. Keep the hours of operation for the places you frequent in a handy place—maybe your car sun visor or glove compartment. This will save you from wasting a ton of time by driving to a store that is closed by the time you get there.

108. Carry a few return address labels in your wallet. Whenever you need to give someone your address you can stick a label on the form and save yourself the time.

109. How many times have you run out to the store only to find out they are out of or don't carry what you are looking for? This is a huge minute muncher. Consider calling ahead. Ask the store to put aside what it is you are coming to purchase.

INSIDER TIP:
Ask the employee their name. This will help ensure they will actually pull the item and save it for you since now you know who they are.

110. Beauty salons and doctors alike tend to run farther behind as their day progresses. If you can grab the first appointment of the day or the first appointment after the lunch break, you have a very good chance of going in on time.

111. Take work with you when you know there is a good chance you'll have a wait. While in the car waiting to pick up a child from sports practice or waiting to go into your appointment or meeting, you can balance your checkbook, write thank-you notes, catch up on your pile of reading material, or even return phone calls. To ensure you have what you need to do the task, pack your in and out tote bag in advance.

INSIDER TIP:
Pack a clip board so you are sure to have a hard writing surface.

112. Do you ever wonder how much time you spend chauffeuring your children and their friends all around town? Many times it does not even pay to drive back home and sit and wait for them. Parents all over are in the same boat. So next time you are standing around with other moms and dads strike up a conversation about carpooling. Most parents will be thrilled to come up with a plan that cuts their driving time down. A little extra work to set it up saves a ton of time in the long run.

113. If you are like most people, you want to be helpful. When asked to pitch in and volunteer, without thinking, do you find yourself blurting out "Sure, no problem," only to feel stressed out and overbooked? If you can take a few months off from volunteering, you can use that time to take care of your home first, and then with everything in order you'll have more time to volunteer and not feel crazed or guilty because you've put others ahead of your own family.

INSIDER TIP:

Practice saying no with phases such as, "Normally I'd love to, but right now I've taken on more than I can handle." Give yourself permission to reconsider a current commitment, volunteer for only one project at a time, or offer to split the role so two people can do half the amount of work.

114. To help avoid volunteer overload, at the start of every season, choose how many volunteer activities you want to be involved in and then seek them out. By choosing where you wish to spend your time you can feel guilt free when asked to pitch in for other things and you can limit the number of directions you are pulled. Wouldn't you rather fill a few positions really well then to skate by on many?

115. Before you say that hiring a house-cleaner is not in your budget, think about whether there is something you do that you'd prefer to exchange for a housecleaner (even if it is every other week or once a month for the heavy cleaning). Do you get a manicure or go out to dinner two or three times a month? Would you trade that in so you didn't have to clean? Your answer may be yes or no. Even if you opt to clean yourself, you still might call in help once or twice a year for spring and fall cleaning.

116. By planning your meals in advance you'll save yourself hours every month. Imagine not stopping at the store to buy ingredients for just one dinner or something you forgot. Don't complicate the meal planning process. Simply ask family members to tell you three or four meals they enjoy. Use this list as a guide and work from there.

117. Make meals in less time by preparing what you can in advance. Chop the vegetables for the stir-fry while you put some in the kid's lunches, or place items in the Crock-Pot to cook later.

118. Ask everyone in the house to pitch in and create a meal or a portion of the meal. Even young children can make sandwiches, microwave meals, or help with easy tasks.

119. Buy prepared or partially prepared food for some parts of the meal and cook the simpler items. For example, you can buy a roasted chicken and make the stuffing. Buy a pie for dessert but add dollops of whipped cream and a sprinkle of cinnamon. The semi-homemade meal is a perfect compromise.

120. Plan to shop once a week at the most. Make one master shopping list of the items you buy most often grouped by category or aisle. Then make fifty-two copies of the list so you can simply highlight what you need to buy. That way there is a central location for listing items that need to be bought instead of incomplete lists jotted down on the backs of envelopes scattered between your house, car, and wallet. Place the list on the refrigerator or on the inside of the pantry cabinet door so everyone in the family can simply check off what is needed.

121. Staple coupons to your shopping list so they are not forgotten. Keep a pen on a string nearby so you can write a "C" next to the item on the list to remind yourself you have a coupon.

122. Instead of shopping when everyone else is at the market, you can avoid long lines, diminished stock, and busy parking lots by shopping off peak hours, like first thing in the morning or later in the evening. You'll receive better service and be in and out much faster.

123. Before you go grocery shopping plan your meals for the next one to two weeks. Once you know what you intend to cook you can compare that to what you have in the house so you know what you need to buy.

124. Before going shopping, decide ahead of time which brands you'll buy if you have a preference; this prevents you having to stand in front of rows of toothpaste trying to pick one.

125. Once you know what you're cooking for the week, write the meals on the family calendar or a kitchen whiteboard. Your family will know what's for dinner, and you won't have to answer the age-old question, "What's for dinner?"

126. Use a chalkboard or whiteboard in the kitchen to list the snacks available. This will ensure the fruit you bought gets eaten and the snacks are used. Create the list as you unpack the groceries to make it simple.

127. When you're cooking a meal that will reheat well, like lasagna, make double and freeze the extra. That way, on a night when time is tight, you can heat that up instead of driving by the fast-food window.

128. Use a slow cooker or a Crock-Pot. They make good meals and take little time. Once you toss the ingredients in that morning, you can let it cook all day and a homemade meal is waiting for you at the end of the day.

129. A great way to save lots of time is to shop from home on your computer or from catalogs. Many online retailers keep your list so you simply have to check off when you want to reorder. Groceries, books, gifts, office supplies, pet supplies, drugstore items, and much more are available online.

INSIDER TIP:

If you are uncomfortable with supplying your credit card to online retailers consider opening one account used only for these purchases to limit the possibility of fraudulent purchases.

130. You can save a tremendous amount of time if you opt for delivery. Think about what you currently run out to get that you can have delivered instead. Your dry cleaning, movies, prescription medications? When you weigh the aggravation of running out along with the gas and time it costs in most cases it makes more sense to take advantage of the convenience.

131. By simply wearing a watch, you can save more time. You will become more aware of how long tasks are taking you. Additionally, you will be better able to keep track of what time it is so you will not run late.

BONUS TIP:
Don't bother setting your clock five minutes ahead to trick yourself. You'll remember you did it and simply subtract five minutes.

132. Another great way to gain lost time is to call a blackout. Turn off the television and computer and hang up the phone. One less hour a week spent in front of a screen equates to a fifty two hours back in your pocket a year! To get family members on board you can make it a pretend black out and eat by candlelight then play games and chat.

133. Setting a timer is one of the best ways to keep from losing valuable time. Set a timer to ring ten minutes before you have to leave so you can finish what you are doing and get ready without having to rush or leave tasks undone. Additionally, you can use the timer to prompt you to switch to another task. You'll be reminded of how long you've been surfing the net or talking to a friend on the phone.

134. By grouping your errands together you can leave the house once and get much more accomplished on one trip. Plan to start with the errand farthest from the house and then work closer until you end up back home. Before you leave be sure to double-check that you have everything you need.

135. Do like tasks together. Make all your phone calls at one time, write out all your bills at one time, and so on. You will be on a roll once you start. Switching to another task could break your momentum.

136. Before leaving for an appointment call ahead and confirm. Check to see if the appointments are running on time or if it has been pushed back. Also, call ahead before going to a restaurant to ask if they provide a wait list.

137. Before driving to the library, call the front desk to see if they have your title. If not, reserve it and have them call you when it comes in.

138. Try not to buy items that will require you to take special care of them. Silver that needs polishing and clothing that needs ironing or hand washing, are good examples of items to think twice about before purchasing.

139. Other special care tasks include time-consuming beauty regimens. Try to work with what is natural, if you have curly hair but like to flat iron it, you might choose to do this only for special occasions. Hair coloring, manicures, and pedicures all fall into this category. The exception to this rule is if you use time in the salon as a stress reliever.

BONUS TIP:
Buff colored nail polish tends to show less chipping which can help you stretch the time between appointments.

140. Splitting your focus between two projects actually takes you longer than focusing on each one individually. Try combining tasks instead. Can you listen to your child read their book report while you sort the laundry? Or can you sit and pay bills while your child does homework at the kitchen table?

141. Stop the zig zag—it is a huge time waster, and this is how it goes; you decide to clear up your bedside table. Before you start you see the glass of water you meant to bring downstairs. You take it to the kitchen, and put it in the dishwasher. While you are there, you decide to run the dishwasher but you are out of soap, so you run downstairs to get a box of detergent. And so on and so on. Before you know it you've been busy all day but the nightstand never got cleared off. Avoid this by simply sticking to the task and making a pile of items to distribute throughout the house once you are done with the original task.

142. You are not the only one who can sort laundry, put away groceries, or load the dishwasher. You are however the only one who can do it exactly your way. Be willing to give up perfection for help. Plus it helps the person who is helping to build their skill set and confidence level.

143. Simply planning a task ahead of time saves countless minutes in the long run. Before setting out to do something take a moment to think it through. Do you have everything you need to complete it? Have you set aside the right amount of time? Do you know what you need to know? If the answer is yes, proceed to success. If not, get what you need before you begin. You'll be glad you did.

144. Program commonly called phone numbers into the speed dial on your home phone, cell phone, and fax machine.

145. For the next week or so wear a watch consistently and watch how long it actually takes you to complete a task. You may think you need only twenty minutes to get ready in the morning, but you may be surprised to see it takes forty, so no wonder you're always running late. On the other hand, you may expect it to take two hours to clean up the playroom but you may be surprised to find it only takes one, especially when others pitch in and help. Knowing how long tasks take allows you to better plan your day.

146. Stop interrupting yourself or allowing others to interrupt you. When you are working on something, allow the phone to go to voice mail, ignore email, and opt to just get the job done.

147. Notice where you lose time by observing how your day flows. You may be surprised to find lost pockets of time. Does opening the mail take an inordinately long amount of time because you do not use a letter opener? Making even one small change can get you minutes back in your day.

148. At the start of each month, take a quick scan of what is coming up so you can prepare in advance. No more pulling that little black dress out of the closet for a wedding in three hours only to remember it needed the seam repaired. Instead, you can now get an idea of the month's events and plan. Do you need special clothing or gifts? Get it on the list now so you have it when you need it. Ensure success with this tip by writing on the calendar where you are placing the item. For example, "birthday party June 13 gift in front hall closet."

9.

Your "To Do" List and Calendar Management

149. You must have a single central location where you are writing down what needs to get done. For you it might be a paper calendar or an electronic handheld device such as a PDA. Which one is right for you? Do you remember things by their color or where you wrote them on a page? Do you like to see your full week or month at a glance? If so then you will most likely work best with a paper calendar. But if you remember events by date, have many recurring events, and are willing to put in the extra effort to keep the batteries charged then an electronic handheld device is most likely a good choice for you.

150. Choose a planner that has every-thing you need. There are so many on the market that you can choose one with the display you prefer. For example, do you like to see your whole month at a glance? Then you need those pages. And remember, some planners are also wallets or have a strap so they can be carried like a purse.

151. Pull out your calendar and pencil in decluttering time. You can't organize in your spare time, because extra time never seems to be there. Pick a weekly block of time and use it for organizing. This routine will keep you from falling behind, especially at the busiest times of the year.

152. Before you begin your new calendar take a moment and enter all major events such as birthdays, anniversaries, school holidays, and other dates to remember. Keep this list paper clipped to the last page of the calendar and use it each time you start a new calendar.

BONUS TIP:
Throughout the year as you add events to the calendar, add them to your master list as well.

153. Whenever you enter an event on the calendar that requires another action, block off time for that action as well. For example, when you write in "wedding" on April 8, block off time to buy the gift a few weeks earlier.

154. Try assigning a colored pen to each member of the family. Then write calendar items in the corresponding colored pen. That way a quick look can tell you who is doing what and when.

155. Create a "to do" basket. Designate a smallish container or basket as the one place where you will store items relating to a task you have to do that week. For example, a package to return to someone you will see in a few days, a book you need to return to the library, and a card you want to mail by the end of the week can all go in the basket.

156. Do you have a time of the day or evening when you feel more alive and productive? You may be a morning person, a night person, or a late afternoon person. Get to know your prime time and choose to do tasks at that time that require more thought, focus, and patience.

157. Between housecleaning, errands, laundry, shopping, and cooking, just caring for the home can feel like a full-time job. To get a handle on all that needs to be accomplished write out a schedule. An example: laundry on Tuesday and Thursday, grocery shopping on Wednesday evening, cleaning on Fridays, and errands on Monday mornings. Post the schedule so everyone in the house will become accustomed to adding items to the grocery list before shopping day, taking laundry to the laundry room prior to laundry day, and asking for an errand to be run on Mondays.

158. Don't schedule things too close together; allot time for traffic accidents, weather delays, someone else running late, and so on.

FAST

Get started fast by recognizing three of the ways you know you tend to lose time. Then make a plan to reclaim that time immediately.

Part Six:

Clutterproofing Essentials

The simple fact is that you can't just organize clutter. Sorry, but you just won't be able to get the result you want. If you keep everything you have and just store it more effectively, all you've done is spent your time, energy, and sometimes money, rearranging items you may never use. This temporary Band-Aid only works for hours, days, or maybe a week. Before you know it, things are back to how they were, or maybe even worse. Before you begin to organize, you need to pare down to just the items you use and love. If that sounds scary, it's not, I promise. I'm going to show you how to start off slow. You will not have to make any earth-shattering decisions or dump stuff before you are ready. We'll go at your pace.

There are truly only three steps to successfully conquering clutter.

Step 1: Sort your stuff "like with like."
Step 2: Put away only what you use and love or what the IRS says you need to keep.
Step 3: Maintain your newly organized space.

When followed exactly, consistently working on one area in small blocks of time, these steps and the strategies in this book will work wonders!

10.

Professional Clutterproofing Strategies

159. Make a plan. You need to know what your desired result is before you can set out to get there.

160. Two-minute rule. One of the easiest and no cost ways to make a dramatic change in your home immediately is by using the two-minute rule. If you can do a task in two minutes or less, do it right then. There are so many things that you put off until later that take such little time you could do them quickly. Hang up a jacket instead of draping it over the back of a chair, put a glass in the sink instead of leaving it for later, RSVP to an invitation, call to make a doctors appointment, and more. With all the little tasks handled and out of the way, your day will run much smoother and there will be less stuff left out around the house.

161. Eighteen-minute blocks of time. There is so much to do on any given day it's unrealistic to think you'll have a huge chunk of time to get organized. Waiting until you have five hours to empty a closet means it most likely will not happen. When is the last time you remember having a uninterrupted five hour block of time? Instead of quantity go for quality and break up a large task into many small blocks of time. Dive into the closet even if you only have eighteen minutes. You'll surprise yourself with how much you accomplish—a top shelf, the first twenty hanging garments, and half the shoes! And how often should you do an eighteen-minute block of time? A minimum of once a week because a short, dedicated, and focused block of time is incredibly powerful.

162. Divide by half. Downsize your stuff by half. For example, if you have thirty books keep only fifteen. Or if you have twelve T-shirts for hanging around the house or exercising, hold onto your favorite six.

163. Put it away ready to use. Never put something away if it is in need of repair or cleaning. If a skirt needs a button or a blanket needs a good washing, do it before you put it away. That way whenever you take some-thing out to use it, you know it will be in working condition ready to be used.

164. Label everything. I can't stress this enough. When things are labeled, it makes life so much easier.

165. Sort into piles. When faced with bunches of stuff to go through simply start by making piles of like items. Once you have piles of like items you can see how much of what you have. You can then sort each pile into keep, toss, donate, pass along, and maybe piles.

166. The maybe pile. This is a great compromise for all the items you think you might be ready to part with but you have a bit of doubt about letting go. Toss them in a pile and revisit them later. To keep yourself from putting everything in the maybe pile, limit yourself to one laundry basket-sized container. When the container nears capacity, stop and pull out some of the maybe items, making room for new ones and making firm decisions about whatever you pull out.

167. When you go back through the pile if you are still undecided then put them in a box. Tape the box shut, write the contents on the outside, and pick a date six to twelve months in the future. Write the date on the box and if by that time you have not had to go to the box to get something then you can let the entire box go.

BONUS TIP:

To ensure that this tip works do not open the box when it the date rolls around. You will only be reminded of all the reasons why you couldn't part with it in the first place and you will probably scratch out the date and write in another future date.

168. Think vertical. This is the single best way to maximize your space. Try slim bookcases that reach floor to ceiling or consider mounting shelves high on a wall to hold decorative items and books. Another way to use your vertical space is to hang things on the wall, such as pans in the kitchen, toys in the playroom, or purses and hats in the bedroom.

169. Have all your supplies ready. To avoid starting and then stopping to run and get something like a trash bag, have everything on hand before you begin.

170. Store it where you use it. This is another basic principle that makes life much easier. If you simply store the items near where you use them, where they naturally fall, you'll do a lot less running around. There's no sense going against the grain.

171. Give everything a home. Each item you own needs a place to live and must be returned there when you are finished using it.

172. Before putting something away take a moment and ask yourself, "Is it worth keeping?" Sometimes we are so programmed to simply put something away we never stop to ask ourselves if we want to keep it. So before you toss an inkless pen back in the pen cup or put a puzzle without all its pieces on the toy shelf, ask yourself, is it worth keeping?

173. Leave ample time to clean up. One sure way to take two steps backwards after taking one step forward is to not leave time to wrap up a job. Maybe you've emptied an area and then been interrupted or have had to leave the project; then everything you've just done gets mixed back together undoing all your hard work. Give yourself time to put everything back before you move on.

174. Prepare yourself for the fact that an area may look worse before it looks better. During the sorting phase, there may be more things out and around. But rest assured that the end result will be well worth it.

175. A wonderful way to part with items you no longer use and love is to pass them along to charity. Choosing one that picks up makes the process especially convenient.

BONUS TIP:

Make a standing appointment with the charity. That way you'll force yourself to have at least one bag ready when they come.

176. Just like any other chore or job, you need to make time to stay organized. Schedule time consistently to maintain the areas you have organized or to start a new clutter-clearing project.

177. Ask questions. How long have I had it? Can I get it again? Does it still work? Do I know how to use it? Does it have all its pieces? When was the last time I used it? Would someone else get more enjoyment from it? What's the worst thing that would happen if I let go of this? Could I live with that? Do I know someone who has it and can lend it to me if needed? Does having it around bring me joy?

178. Give yourself a realistic deadline and stick to it. Without a deadline, plans can take forever to get accomplished. Choose a self-imposed deadline for when you want to complete the entire project. Then, work backwards and write in smaller incremental deadlines on the calendar for accomplishing parts of the larger task.

179. Get things up and out. Whenever you have something ready to go, a bag of trash, a bin of recycling, a container for charity, or a pile of items to pass along to others, get it out of the house to the curb or in the car so you can free up valuable space.

180. When a common task is continually left undone, stop and consider why. For example, if freshly washed laundry is always left in the baskets maybe its because the drawers or closets are too jam-packed to put more clothes in. The solution is usually easier than you may think.

181. If you feel compelled to pass along items to friends or family members then designate one place to collect them. The next time you are due to see the person note on the calendar a simple reminder to take the items with you.

11.

Handling Sensitive Clutter Challenges

182. Lost loved ones stuff. When someone close to you passes away, their belongings can trigger all sorts of memories of that person. Sometimes, even things we know are trash become sentimental. I suggest you wait one year before making decisions about the items. After that time passes, choose the items you will actually use, pick some items for display, select a couple for a keepsake memory box, take photos of anything you are not keeping but that was meaningful at one time, and pass along the rest. The solution is to keep in mind that your memories of that person are in your mind, not in the stuff they once owned. You may also find it helpful to have a close friend or family member sit with you as you sort through the items.

BONUS TIP:
It may help to get creative. For example, you can take some of their favorite clothing and have a quilt or pillow sewn from it.

183. Abandoned family items. When family members leave items in your home for you to care for, you have every right to ask them to take the items back, whether it is a child who has moved out or a sibling who has asked you to temporarily store something. Your home is not a storage facility. The easiest way to do this without hurt feelings is to set a date with the person by which they need to either come to take the items or send you the money to have them shipped to them. If the items are not removed by that date, you can feel good about passing the items to a charity where they will actually be used.

184. Gifts you received but do not love. Whether it is not your size or just not your taste, you are the new owner of it. After you say thank you for the thoughtful gift it is your choice what to do with it from then on. You can opt to pass it along to someone who will use and love it. The key is to remember that the giver would prefer that you pass the gift along then be burdened with it. Would you rather tuck the gift away in a pile of clutter and stress about it, or let it go and be useful to someone else. Most of the time, the giver would like the gift to be used, even if it is not by you.

185. Future or past ideas. Often we own things that interested us at one time or that we plan to get to in the future. The problem is that our tastes and interests change often. It is common to keep things like art projects you might do one day or a box of love letters from an old flame. The problem is that doing so keeps us rooted in the past or living in the future. The solution is to decide to live in the present. Keep and buy only what interests you right now.

186. Passing items down from child to child. It is nice to pass items along from one child to another. It can certainly save money, and it allows you to get more use out of items one child loved. The challenge is to remember that you have it when you need it and to find a safe place to stash it in the meantime. The solution is to choose carefully what should be kept for future use. As you decide what to hold on to, weigh the pros and cons of keeping larger items that require a large amount of storage space. Sometimes using the space for the next few months or years is worth more than rebuying an item. Store items cleanly and correctly so they are still usable when you pull them out of storage. Label everything and create a master list that you can refer to. If the item was difficult to use or does not have all its pieces then you might opt to let the item go.

Store items by age group so you can easily pull out the items as the child grows.

187.

The item may be worth something someday. If trying to keep the item long enough for it to become valuable makes you feel overwhelmed, is it worth it? Remember that when you are finally ready to sell it, you also have to find someone willing to pay for it, or it is not worth anything. If you are going to hold onto it, do the research to be sure it will be a collector's piece. Read an antique guide, consult an appraiser, or search online auction sites to see who is really paying for what you own. The truth is that often you only think it is worth something, so it is merely a perceived value. If you love it enough to use it or display it now, do so. Otherwise, do the research to see if it is worth keeping or pass it along to someone who will use and love it now.

188.

Collections. Items in a collection are only worth something if they are displayed in a way that allows you to enjoy them. Having them packed away in storage does not give you the opportunity to enjoy them. So pull your collectibles out of storage, choose your favorites and display those. The solution is to avoid letting the collection grow so large that it outgrows the space you have. You should either deem your collection complete and let family members know so they do not buy you any more items for it, or create a list of the items that you still need to make the collection complete. That way you don't buy or get pieces that you don't really want.

BONUS TIP:

You do not have to have every possible item in the collection for the collection to be complete, you just need to have the ones you like. Remember, it is okay to let a collection go if it no longer is enjoyable.

12.

The Golden Rules of Storage

189. Clear boxes are best for storing items since it is easy to see what you have inside.

190. When storing items, be sure to label all sides of the container, including the top. This way when you are searching for the container, it can be spotted easily.

191. If you prefer not to write directly on the storage container, simply stick a piece of clear packing tape to the box, and then write on the tape. If you change the contents of the container, you can simply pull off the tape instead of crossing out your original writing.

192. Before you buy any container to store items in, the first step is to measure what needs to be stored and the area you have to store it in. No sense going out and buying a bookcase, only to return home to find out you have more books than will fit or that the bookcase is too tall to fit in your room.

193. You are going to get more stuff, so always leave room to grow. If you are shopping for a storage tub for your out of season clothing, be sure to get one a little larger then you need at the time. This way, when you are given a sweater as a gift or you buy yourself another jacket, it will fit in storage.

194. Store like with like. This is vital to your success. Place like items with like items. If you place all sorts of unrelated items together, it makes it much more difficult to find things. So for example, place all your cookbooks on one shelf of the bookcase or in one area of your kitchen. If you leave some in the home office and some in the dining room, you will never know which ones are where or how many you own.

195. For your storage to work best, it must be easy to reach. Do not store your everyday dishes in the cabinet over the refrigerator that you need a stepladder to get to. Place your commonly used items in the easiest-to-reach places.

196. The only way you'll know where your stuff is stored is if you make the storage areas easy to remember. For example, placing gifts to give away in a bin under your bed might get them out of sight but will you remember where you put them? If not, it is not the best place to keep them.

197. Everything you own has to have a place to be put away—even the pending papers, like party invitations. Tabletops, countertops, and the floor are not options.

198. As confusing as it may be to have no home for your things, it can be even more confusing to have multiple homes for things. Whenever you need something, it could be in one of many places, and you waste lots of time searching. Stop the searches by having only one place to look for things.

199. The exception to the one home rule is if you tend to need things in different areas of your home. If that is the case then multiples will save you time. For example, if you stored scissors in just one place, you'd always be running there to get them. Instead, have multiples and store them where you use them. Maybe one in your dresser drawers to cut tags off clothing, one pair in the kitchen, a few pairs with the kids' arts and crafts supplies, and a pair in the garage.

200. Whenever you have more of anything than what you need at a time, like if you prefer to buy in bulk, then you should store the extra in an overflow spot. For example, if you buy six tubes of toothpaste at once, twenty-four rolls of paper towels, or a box of pens at a time, you cannot store it all where you use it. If you did that, you'd have six open tubes of toothpaste at once, no room to move by the paper towels and bottles of Wite-Out filling a single desk drawer. Instead, designate one area for the overflow. Then instead of running to the store to stock up you can shop at home. So, put out one tube of toothpaste for use and store the overflow in a labeled bin in the linen closet. Place a few spare rolls of paper towels in the pantry and stash the overflow in another place like metal shelving in the basement. And take one bottle of Wite-Out and put it in the desk drawer, then store the overflow with other home office supplies to restock the desk as needed.

FAST
Get started fast by choosing one of the above techniques and putting it into place immediately.

Part Seven:

Room by Room: Applying the Tips in Your Home

Once you have sorted your stuff and pared down to just what you use and love, it is time for step two: put away only what you use and love or what the IRS says you need to keep. Everything you own needs a place to live, no exceptions. Choose a home that is easy to reach and simple to remember.

When organizing a room, store items where you use them. To do this most effectively you should think about the activities that take place in each room. When you know how the room needs to function it will make it easier to identify what needs to be stored there.

Lastly, as you identify what storage supplies you need to store items, look around your home. Chances are you already have something that will work. You might also consider repurposing an item of furniture, for example, a dresser may not work in a bedroom but might make a great sideboard in the dining room. If you don't have what you need, then you'll want to purchase the item, just be sure to measure first, nothing is worse than buying something and getting home only to find out it is not the right size.

Now it's time to put these key strategies into action. Don't be overwhelmed wondering where to begin. Simply choose one area to focus on first and start there. One you start the ball rolling it will be easier to keep moving. The key is just to get started.

13

Entryway

201. Everyone in the house needs a place to put their stuff on their way in the door. Be it backpacks, briefcases, shoes, or umbrellas, there is a way to avoid having the floor be the family dumping ground. Simply designate a space for each person in the house. No matter how young, infants usually have the most amount of stuff. Label the area with the person's name and have that be his or her own personal dumping ground. This is also where you can keep bags you use often or on a regular basis, like a gym bag or a tote with the nail polishes you need when going to the salon.

202. No mudroom? No problem. If your house is not equipped with a mudroom, you can create one by simply converting a hall closet. Empty out the closet and place hooks on the inside of the door (if you have young children place the hooks low). Then add a rack for shoes and baskets for smaller accessories. Guest's coats can also find a home in the makeshift mudroom, plus top shelves can be used for storage and out of season items.

203. Don't want to use a closet as your makeshift mudroom? Try placing an armoire in or near the entryway. The doors can still hold hooks and the shelving and hanging space will be much appreciated. If adding an armoire would make the walkway too narrow, see if it is possible to recess the armoire into the wall.

204. Another alternative to the no mudroom dilemma is to place a baker's rack in the entryway. The shelves and cabinets should do the trick.

205. Another solution is to add a chest of drawers. Although not as functional because it does not allow for hanging space, it still solves many of the entryway issues.

206. By adding a bench to the entryway, you gain not only storage space in the lift up seat, but extra seating as well. Having a seat nearby is handy as you try to put shoes on children.

207. To avoid walking out the door without the necessary items such as mail, cell phone, and papers for a meeting, try the "don't forget me" door hanger. Simply secure a plastic shoe holder to the back of the door and label the pockets with such categories as keys, mail, phone, umbrella, and so on. The next time you walk out the door you can't help but grab the items and take them with you.

BONUS TIP:

If you tend to leave the house without your cell phone because it is charging, place the phone in your bag while it's charging. Then simply unplug it and go when you grab your purse on your way out the door.

208. A slim line table with drawers can be a great addition to the entryway. Each drawer can be a home to a specific item, such as keys, wallets, loose change, and incoming bills. Plus it can double as a spot for larger outgoing items so you can't help but see them on your way out the door.

209. Shoe trays are the best way to keep muddy and wet shoes from dripping on your floor. They come in a variety of styles, so there is sure to be one that matches your décor.

210. Try placing a coat tree in the hallway to easily collect all the coats for family and guests. Placing a short coat tree next to it so children can hang their own coats without assistance.

211. Give your keys a permanent home and you will never have to hunt for them again. You can hang them on a hook at the entryway, place them in a decorative bowl, or designate one small drawer for keys only.

212. To avoid confusion later over what keys belong to what, label the keys now. That way later you'll know whether or not you need the key because you'll know exactly what it belongs to. Label the keys using codes that only you understand in case the keys end up in the wrong hands.

213. A large decorative vase, container, or your typical umbrella stand makes a great decorative statement in the entryway and is useful on rainy days when you have a wet umbrella to put away. This can be the permanent home for the umbrellas or you can hang them on a nail on the inside of the hall closet.

TOSS

No-brainer toss list: Keys that have no known purpose, outdated mail, shoes that are too small or grungy, broken umbrellas, and coats that do not fit anyone in the house.

14.

Kitchen

214. Short on wall space for a message center? Paint a cabinet door, inside or out, with magnetic metallic or blackboard paint or tack on cork tiles for a no fuss message center.

215. Make sure your message center offers a separate section per family member. That way there is a place to leave each other messages.

216. Have people in the house be responsible for clearing their messages daily or weekly. Your new house rule might be: in our home, before we have dessert we clear our message center of outdated messages.

217. The space over the window below the ceiling is not that convenient of a storage space for items needed often. But it is perfect for storing decorative items, or rarely used items.

218. To keep the recipe in sight while cooking you can use a pull down cookbook rack. This eliminates the need for a cookbook rack that is always out on the countertop.

219. To hide unsightly countertop appliances you can place them in an "appliance garage." If you do not have one built into your cabinets already then you can make your own by placing a decorative box upside down over the group of appliances.

220. Decide that this week you will learn how to operate any appliance you do not know how to use or you will let it go.

221. To avoid having your large glass bowls clanking against each other as you open large, deep drawers, use a pegboard organizer. The pegboard lays flat on the bottom of the drawer. Then tall pegs slip into the slots acting as dividers to keep items from touching each other.

222. A great way to organize pots and pans, especially if you are short on cabinet space, is to hang them from a pot rack.

BONUS TIP:
Many newer style pot racks also have a light so they do double duty.

223. Take oversized bags of snacks and separate them into smaller baggies. This takes up less space in the pantry, makes it easier to grab and go, and stops us from eating the entire large bag.

BONUS TIP:
Store the bags of munchies in an easy to get to basket or in a single deep drawer so you can literally grab and go.

224. Try this new rule—in our house, we only eat in the kitchen or dining room.

225. For meals that need to be cleaned up fast consider using paper dishes.

BONUS TIP:
If you have just cleaned the kitchen you might also choose to use paper products so the kitchen can stay clean for at least a few hours.

226. Some kitchen gadgets are just more trouble then they are worth. Don't feel an obligation to use the newest gadget to cook with; sometimes the old fashioned way is the best. If it is difficult to clean, operate, has too many pieces, or you have another way of doing the task, then you can part with the item.

227. Separate the kitchen into zones for the functions you will perform there: food storage, preparation, cooking, baking, serving, and clean up. Once you know what area will serve for what task, it will be easy to store the tools you need nearby.

228. Cabinets, a pantry area, the refrigerator, and freezer are where the food is stored. Remember to keep like with like in all these areas, even in the refrigerator and freezer.

229. Designate an area of the kitchen to be the preparation area. If you are short on counter space then consider using a rolling cart. You'll want to have easy access to the garbage, a faucet, and the places where you keep marinades, mixing bowls, and utensils.

230. Designate another section of the kitchen to be the cooking area. This area should be closer to the stove and allow you easy access to things like pots, pans, knives, cutting boards, wooden spoons, pot holders, cookbooks, cookbook stand, cooking oils, vinegars, herbs, and spices.

BONUS TIP:
Potholders store easily on the inside of a cabinet door hanging on a hook from their loops.

231. In your baking area keep the equipment like the mixing bowls, baking sheets, muffin tins, cake pans, pie plates, measuring spoons and cups, spatulas and wooden spoons. Also have on hand commonly called for ingredients such as flour, white and brown sugar, baking soda and powder, shortening, cocoa, food coloring, extracts, baking chips, and sprinkles.

232. Once dishes are prepared, having a serving zone is helpful. Keep the glasses, flatware, dishes, serving bowls, plates, and serving utensils nearby.

233. Once the meal is over it is nice to be able to wrap up the leftovers and clean up easily. Store Tupperware, plastic wrap, foil, baggies, chip clips, and other storage containers in this area.

BONUS TIP:

For easy clean up of dry spills keep a handheld vacuum charging nearby. You won't have to drag out the large vacuum and children love to use the little vacuums, so let them.

234. If you pack lunches then creating a lunch packing area makes sense. Keep thermoses, brown bags, notepaper for "just because" notes, baggies, and lunch money or tickets in this area.

235. Organize your cooking routine by gathering everything you will need before you begin. This will make it easier to cook but it will also stop you from getting halfway through a recipe only to find out you are missing something and cannot complete the job.

236. Store cookie cutters by category and label each container. Store holiday cookie cutters in the box with the decorations for that holiday or season.

237. Don't clip coupons for brands you do not normally purchase. Buying something you won't or don't use is not a savings.

238. Kids' plastic dishes are such odd shapes; it is easier to keep them in their own cabinet rather than mixing them in with the other dishes.

BONUS TIP:
Move kid-friendly stuff to an "I'll get it myself" shelf lowered for them so they can help themselves.

239. Sippy cups and their lids can be a challenge to keep track of. First, keep only the ones that have all their pieces, are in good working order, and are easy to clean. Then store them in their own bin, in a cabinet, or in a holiday ornament tray. The ornament tray is a plastic tray with twelve slots; each slot holds a cup along with its lid perfectly.

240. Tupperware can make a mess of any cabinet. First, set out all the pieces you have and toss stray lids, containers without lids, and pieces that are too stained or melted. Next, keep only what you will realistically use. A variety of sizes and shapes should stay in the cabinet; you can store the spares in another place. Place all the lids in a lid organizer that attaches to the inside of a cabinet door and nest the Tupperware bowls inside each other.

241. Another Tupperware option is to use a product called the Smart Spin which attaches to any cabinet and spins completely around. It stacks a variety of sizes of containers and their lids in one easy to reach location. The downside to this is that you have to use the containers that come with the product only and it does not accommodate any other sizes.

242. Designate one shelf in the kitchen as the beverage center. There you can place travel mugs, mugs, sugar, tea bags, coffee filters, and anything else you need when grabbing a drink on the run. If you make a shelf near the sink, it makes it easy to rinse spills.

243. Hang a wrap organizer on the inside of a cabinet door to hold cling wrap, aluminum foil, baggies, and rolls of wax and parchment paper.

244. Make serving breakfast a snap by creating a breakfast bin. In the bin you can place all the items you usually need for serving breakfast: bowls, sugar, spoons, and so on. When you go to set up for the meal just bring the bin to the table.

245. A great way to create a ton of space in the kitchen immediately is to toss any large appliances that you do not use such as cotton candy makers, ice cream makers, s'more makers, popcorn poppers, and so on.

246. Clearing the counters of rarely used small appliances is a great way to gain valuable counterspace. If you use the blender once or twice a year, why not put it away and stop having to clean around it.

247. Instead of stacking plates in a cabinet, a more efficient way to store them is on end in slots. You can have a single slotted cabinet installed if you want.

248. To maximize cabinet space use the gap between the bottom of one shelf and the tallest items on the next shelf. Slip on an under-shelf basket and gain instant storage.

249. Slide out shelves can be installed in almost any cabinet. They allow you to reach the back of the shelf easily.

250. Mug trees or hooks screwed in underneath a cabinet are a perfect place to store commonly used mugs.

251. If your pantry area is too small or nonexistent then you can add a rolling pantry. One rolling pantry option is a tall, thin, stack of shelves on wheels. It is only ten inches wide so it can easily roll into small spaces, like the gap between your refrigerator and wall. The five shelves can hold a variety of items including cereal boxes, and once it is rolled into place it blends in with the kitchen and looks like just another cabinet.

252. Still at a loss for a pantry? Try placing an armoire in or near the kitchen. The shelves and drawers will offer plenty of space to stash even the big items.

253. An over the door, hanging pantry is another way to maximize space. This piece simply hangs over the back of a door or can be screwed into the door. The shelves are adjustable and deep enough to hold cans and boxes.

If your door does not have a large enough gap to allow you to hang the pantry, you can screw it to the door instead.

254. When stacking items in your pantry be sure to keep the littlest items in the front or they will be lost behind the taller items.

255. You can store packets such as dry soup mix and seasonings in a durable plastic pouch stuck to the inside of a cabinet door for storage. Or you can attach to the door the large plastic clips made specifically to hold the packets.

256. Take the seasonal items out of your kitchen and store them away. Just by taking out the holiday bake ware, summer serving dishes, smoothie maker, and more, you'll gain valuable kitchen storage space. You can either store all the kitchen stuff in one place, or store the holiday related items in the holiday bins.

257. Large bags of flour, gallon jugs of oils, and oversized boxes of cereal can be difficult to pour. By filling a smaller container from a larger one, you can make it easier to use. Plus, the smaller containers can be easier to store in the kitchen and simply refilled as needed.

258. Make getting things out of the refrigerator a snap by grouping like items together. In one area of the refrigerator, you can place all the drinks, and in another area place all the leftovers. Place all the condiments in a bin, so you can lift out the entire container and use what you need (while preparing a sandwich, for example) then put them all back at once.

BONUS TIP:

Use another bin for marinades. Line that one with paper towels to avoid sticky drips or place each bottle in a paper muffin cup.

259. Place a lazy Susan in the center of your table and fill it with commonly needed items such as napkins, salt, and pepper, so these items can be reached by anyone with a simple spin.

260. Label the shelves in the pantry. It takes just a little while and it saves tons of time in the long run. It will be easy to see what is missing and it allows anyone to put things away since they'll know exactly where everything goes.

261. Make it a rule to clean out the refrigerator and freezer once a month.

262. Store onions and garlic in panty hose to avoid having the skins fall all over the place.

263. Hang cutting boards on the wall, this option takes up no cabinet space and adds flair to the room.

264. Each kitchen is allotted one junk drawer. Add a junk drawer organizer and designate one space per item in the drawer.

265. Hang a plastic bag holder in the kitchen where you can store plastic shopping bags. Since the holder stores over fifty bags, when the holder is full you can recycle the rest of the bags knowing that you have enough on hand.

266. When storing containers that can be messy if they leak, place them in a pan to contain the mess. A small container can hold marinades in the refrigerator and a large dishpan can hold messy cleaners under the sink.

267. When you change the liner bag on the garbage can, toss a few extra bags in the bottom of the can for easy changes in the future.

268. Designate one container for loose change. Empty the container and cash in the change once in awhile for treat money.

269. To gain more shelf space you can hang spray bottles by their handles on a rod above the shelf and out of the way.

270. To help keep placemats organized, store them in a slim under the shelf basket in a cabinet.

271. Most spices have only a six-month shelf life. Mark the date on the bottle when you open it so you always know your spices are fresh.

272. Spices come in containers of such varying shapes and sizes that the standard spice rack does not usually hold all your favorites. Therefore choosing an alterative or an additional organizing piece is usually necessary. Spice racks now come as options in most cabinet designs, but if you are not remodeling your kitchen then a less expensive option is probably more your style. A drawer-based tiered organizer where the spice lay face up may work, as may an expandable three-tiered shelf in a cabinet, or an over-the-door spice rack can hang on a cabinet door.

273. Most spice bottles fit well into a medicine cabinet. Hanging a cabinet meant for the bathroom in the kitchen may be the perfect solution for the spices.

274. Don't alphabetize the spices. Instead, group them by use and place the most commonly used ones in front. For example, you may keep cream of tarter, cinnamon, and vanilla in one area for baking and have another section for marinating spices.

275. Toolbox. Make little jobs easier by keeping a stash of commonly used tools in the kitchen. A hammer, pliers, scissors, and a selection of screwdrivers can be tucked in a drawer or kept in a small toolkit in the cabinet.

276. Keep a pair of scissors in the kitchen. They are a huge time-saver when opening bags, cutting scallions, or opening bakery boxes tied with strings. (And they're safer for these jobs than a kitchen knife.)

277. Batteries are a commonly lost item in a junk drawer. You can stop wasting money on rebuying batteries if you purchase a battery organizer. This piece will hold up to fifty batteries and some models have a battery tester right on them. Put one by the kids' toys in the garage as well.

278. If take-out menus from restaurants are crammed in drawers and hard to find you might consider placing them all in a single folder labeled "Menus." Or you can use a slim three ring binder, slip in a few page protectors and then slide one menu into each page. This way they are protected and can always be found.

BONUS TIP:
Create a duplicate binder of take-out menus and keep it in the car so you can call in an order on your way home.

279. Clip coupons for the restaurants on the take-out menus so when you call to order you remember you have them.

280. You can gain 50 percent more cabinet space when you add shelf extenders—wire pieces designed to withstand over sixty pounds. There are specific ones created to hold entire sets of china in half the space the set would normally take up.

281. Stop clipping coupons if you spend time cutting them out but then never use them.

282. Coupons are only useful if you remember to take them to the store. A great solution is to use a conventional coupon organizer in an unconventional way. Instead of separating the coupons by category, you can separate them by store. As discount coupons come in the mail or you clip them out of the newspaper, you can add them to the appropriate store's section. Then the next time you are in the store you'll have them all with you, especially helpful if you make an unexpected stop.

283. A can dispenser on a shelf in your refrigerator or cabinet is a simple way to gain back lost space. Fill it with cans from the top and they roll out the front; each holds twenty or more cans of various sizes: soup, tuna, soda, and more. No more teetering stacks of cans, and no more searching. Knowing what you are running low in is a breeze.

284. If you have household pets then you know that finding a place to store their food can be an issue. Designate one area for pet food. Then place the food and other necessities in clearly labeled bins. Taking a few moments to pour dog food from a bag into a plastic bin is worth it because getting the food out is so much less of a hassle.

285. Hang the frozen storage reference chart near the freezer. That way on a monthly basis when you clean out the freezer you can easily see what should be kept and what is due to be tossed.

286. Kitchen drawers can commonly become so full you have to push items down in order to open them. To avoid that you'll want to place drawer organizers in every drawer. They have become so popular that they now come in enough styles and colors that you can surely find one that matches your kitchen. Utensils, knives, spices, and junk all have specially designed types.

287. Other drawer organizers can be custom created. By simply buying interlocking pieces you can create a piece that meets your specific needs. With an organizer installed every time you open the drawer, the items stay in place instead of becoming a jumble in the back of the drawer.

288. Garbage cans are a must in the kitchen. You'll want to be sure that the one you are using is large enough and easy to operate. You might be surprised to learn you can cut down on the number of times you have to bag the garbage and bring it out by simply using a larger can that can hold you over a day or two longer. And you can cut down on washing the outside of the can if it is a style that can be opened without touching it with messy hands.

289. If you prefer not to see the garbage you can install one on rails that rolls out from a cabinet only when you need it. You can also use this option for recycling.

290. Try using two garbage cans, one emptied more often for perishables.

291. Since many towns now mandate that you recycle, many companies make attractive options for storing used cans, old newspapers, and empty bottles until recycling day. Attractive units that from the outside look like kitchen hutches or butcher block islands double as recycling storage.

292. If you prefer to store your recycling in the garage area, the same units are also available in plastic. And to avoid having to step out into the garage to toss out the recycling you might choose to add a shelf right outside the door to hold the bins so tossing is easy.

293. If you live in an area where tying up your newspapers is required, then a rack with the twine already attached and a cup for scissors might be the way for you to go.

294. Try storing your cookbooks in another room, such as the dining room.

DOUBLE BONUS TIP:

Check the books out of the library, try them and buy only the ones you like. Or buy a cookbook both you and a friend want, then share it.

295. Clipping a bunch of recipes out and tucking them away does not allow you access to them so you can actually cook them. For easy reference set up an index box with tabbed dividers, one per category, such as breads, salads, casseroles, desserts, and so on. As you clip a new recipe out, tape it to an index card and file it for easy reference.

TRIPLE BONUS TIP:
Tape commonly prepared recipes to the inside of the cabinet door. To keep them clean you can laminate them. Also post a paper showing cooking equivalents for easy reference.

296. Another option for storing recipes or coupons is photo boxes. Label each with a broad category and stack them, you can even let them show since photo boxes are decorative. Then as you clip out recipes or coupons, tuck them into the correct box.

297. You can place recipes in a magnetic photo album (the kind with the plastic peel back page and sticky lines on it). If your recipes are two sided you can use a three ring binder with page protectors inside. Simply slide the recipe into the pocket.

298. A typical address Rolodex is another simple way to store recipes. Take out the A–Z tabs and relabel them with the category names, appetizers, drinks, casseroles, and so on. Then as you get a new recipe, you can staple it onto a Rolodex card and file it in your Recipe Rolodex.

299. A tabletop recipe box is the best option. This option is best if you tend to clip and store many new recipes a week. Use a desktop file box that accommodates hanging folders. Label each folder with a category, soups, main dishes (chicken), main dishes (pork), and so on. Then as you get a new recipe place it in the correct hanging folder. When the folders get thick, you can transfer the recipes into a box or weed some out.

300. An accordion folder is another easy way to store recipes. Label each tab with a recipe category.

BONUS TIP:

Choose just one way to store recipes. As chaotic as it may be not to have a system, it can be even more chaotic to have more than one way.

301. To keep a recipe visible while you are cooking use a tabletop photo clip. The heavy base sits on the table or counter and the clip on the top of the pole holds the recipe.

302. Choose to try one new recipe a week from the clippings. Keep the recipes you like and toss the rest. It is the only way to weed through the pile

303. When you find a recipe you'd like to try in a cookbook, flag the page with a sticky note sticking on the edge. Then write the name of the recipe on the part of the sticky note that shows to make the recipe easy to find later.

304. Lazy Susans in cabinets, countertops, and refrigerators are a perfect way to give yourself access to a variety of items with out having to move anything out of your way to reach.

305. Whenever you make a few different types of sandwiches for an occasion, cut the bread for each type of sandwich in a specific way to differentiate them from one another. For example, no crust on peanut butter and jelly, cut the bread diagonally on the tuna and make squares for the ham and swiss cheese. Another option is to stick different color toothpicks in the sandwiches to tell them apart.

306. Vitamins and other supplements come in bottles varying in size and shape. If you reach for them daily or more often you might opt to place them in a decorative basket or container on the countertop. Alternately, you might spend a few minutes weekly or monthly to place the pills into a pill organizer.

307. Many cabinets are chock full of glass-ware. Is yours? If so you might think about how many people use the glasses and when. It is very possible you can move some to a box and store them for when you are entertaining, giving you much needed daily living space. And as you are boxing some up, you may come across mugs that were a give away or other glassware that you can part with and send to charity.

308. If a cabinet is dim inside, add a light. A lighted cabinet makes it easier to see what is inside and also makes it more difficult to clutter up since you can easily see where things belong.

309. Hang one or two of your more deco-rative mugs from hooks mounted under the cabinets to reach them easily.

310. Remember to fill the coffee maker every night. Whether or not it goes on automatically, it will be one less thing to do in the morning. If you do not have a coffeemaker with an automatic timer, you can place a vacation timer on the outlet so coffee is ready when you wake up.

311. For other mugs that take up valuable cabinet space you might consider a slip on mug rack. They hold six to twelve mugs and slip onto shelves so you can hang them above shorter items and not use shelf space.

312. Finding a pot lid can also be another matching game. A wire rack with slots is one solution; lids sit sideways and you simply pull out the one you need. Pot lid racks also come in a pull out option where you can slide out the drawer and choose your lid.

313. Equally frustrating can be having to take a few pots out of the cabinet just to get to the one you want which is stacked on the bottom. You can add a tiered pot rack that allows you to place one pot per slot with no more stacking.

314. Line the vegetable and fruit bins of the refrigerator with paper towels; they will absorb moisture and make for very easy clean up.

315. When you purchase chicken or meat from the store, place it on a plate to prevent the leaking juices from dripping onto the refrigerator shelves.

316. Do you tend to entertain often, or only a few times a year? Unless you need your platters, serving bowls, and extra silverware out all the time you might consider storing them in the dining room or the basement. Placing them in a clearly marked large container or box can allow you much more room to store your everyday items.

317. If you have the added convenience of a dishwasher then you'll want to be in the habit of putting the dishes directly in the dishwasher. In addition, if you wash dishes by hand keep in mind it takes far less time to wash them immediately before the food sticks. Keeping your sink clear also sets the tone for the cleanliness of the entire kitchen.

318. The like with like rule applies in the kitchen as well. Group all the similar items together. Put all the silverware in one drawer, all the pots in one cabinet, and even in the pantry group like items together. All the canned vegetables together, all the pasta together, and so on.

319. The kitchen most often doubles as the household command center. This is where the mail generally is placed, children's backpacks are emptied, and so on. Create a mini office for yourself in the kitchen. You do not need a desk. Instead, opt for a rolling cart that can be rolled behind closed doors when company arrives.

320. Another option for a mini home office in the kitchen is an armoire. It has great versatility and the doors can be closed when it's not in use.

321. Use the prime real estate in your drawers. Place commonly used items in the front of the drawers and lesser-used items towards the back where it is more difficult to reach. The typical way is to place all the commonly used items in the top drawer. But it is actually easier to reach the front of the top two drawers then the back of the first.

322. Notices and schedules can be posted for easy reference. Instead of plastering the front of your refrigerator with these items, try gluing a piece of cork to the inside of a cabinet door, painting a section with chalkboard paint, or hanging up a small magnetic or whiteboard.

323. When stocking your shelves add the new items to the back so you use the older items first.

324. Keep scoops in containers of sugar, flour, powdered drink mixes, and coffee so you don't always have to search for one.

325. If the original packaging is airtight and you are going to use the food right away then leave it in its packaging. However, items in flimsy bags or that you are not going to use right away should be transferred into airtight containers.

BONUS TIP:
When you do this tear off the cooking directions and store them in the new container.

326. Add more storage space to the kitchen instantly by hanging an over-the-door plastic shoe bag. Each pocket—meant for shoes—works well for snack bars, shake mixes, seasoning packets, and other small items that tend to get lost on shelves.

327. Dating the items in the kitchen may sound a little over the top. But if you've ever served expired salad dressing or wondered when you bought the mayonnaise then it makes a lot of sense. It only takes a moment if you have a permanent marker on hand. Use Velcro to stick one to the side of the refrigerator. You'll always have the marker at hand.

BONUS TIP:
If you don't want the marker on your refrigerator then place it on the inside of the pantry door or in the junk drawer.

328. If you have an overabundance of wooden spoons or other utensils then pare down. You can give the duplicates to a charity so someone who needs them can use them now, or you can box them up and store them elsewhere. Then when you need a replacement you can shop at home first.

329. Lots of space under your sink is usually lost to the pipes that are there. To maximize the space use a slate shelf that adjusts to fit around your pipes.

330. Creating a simple recycling center is a great way to deal with all the recyclables. There are a few options. You can take drawers out of the kitchen cabinets, replace them with baskets, line the baskets, and use one basket per type of recyclable item. Another option is to purchase a premade recycling center; they are usually tall and slender, with removable bins to unload the recyclables. One other choice if you have an attached garage is to set up the containers in there. Place the containers right by the door so you can open the door and toss them right in.

TOSS

No-brainer toss list: Tupperware too stained or without its lid, expired coupons, broken dishes, expired or outdated foods.

15.

Dining Room

331. To help keep your tablecloths from wrinkling, fold them over a pants hanger and hang them in the closet.

332. Place serving trays and oversized dishes in the sideboard. This keeps them out of the way and easy to reach as needed. Another way to store these items is to prop them on a shelf. This is a great solution if they are decorative and compliment your décor.

333. Don't have a bar area? You can create one by storing all the necessities like bar glasses, bowls for nuts, and shot glasses in an armoire. A slender armoire works well, and it is especially helpful if it has a pull out drawer that you can use for mixing drinks and as a buffet when entertaining. Screw a slotted rack upside down under the top shelf and glasses can be stored by their stems. You can hang towels and other necessities on the inside of the doors. Wine and other liquor bottles tuck away neatly in the bottom cabinet of the armoire.

BONUS TIP:
This is also the best storage place for drink recipe books.

334. Another option for a bar is a rolling cart or wall-mounted bar. A rolling cart allows you to roll out the cart when needed and then roll it back into a corner when not in use. And if you have a tall table and a low cart, the cart might roll right underneath to tuck out of sight. The wall-mounted bars affix to the wall and have slots to slip in glasses and a few openings for bottles.

335. Designate one drawer in the side bar as the candle drawer. Store candles, matches, casual candlesticks, and snuffers. Display more decorative, delicate candlesticks in the china cabinet.

336. Once you've selected the few flower vases you are going to hold onto see if any of them nest inside each other. Any time you can nest something it saves a ton of space. Then store them on one shelf in the sidebar. If any of the vases are particularly decorative or sentimental then you may choose to display them in the china cabinet.

337. You have a few choices about how to store your china. You can stow it away in china protectors and store it in the attic, basement, or garage. You can display it in your china cabinet, or you can start to use and enjoy it. A good compromise is to store away two place settings to use in the future. If you have children, you can keep two complete sets protected to use when they have left home. In the meantime, display the pieces of the china set that you would not use all that often, like gravy boats and butter trays. Then use the rest of the set. It makes a meal more special and allows you to use the special pieces that have tradition and tell your family's history.

338. Keep napkins and other items needed for mealtime, like salt and pepper, in the dining room instead of continually toting them from the kitchen to the dining table. To make serving a breeze, place food on a tray and carry it into the dining room in one trip.

339. Instead of cramming all the display items into the china cabinet, select a few to put on display storing the others in the cabinet. Every season you can rotate the display case. To help make your cabinet professionally staged notice how high-end stores display their items, and then duplicate it in your own home.

340. If you have a few party items like birthday candles, streamers, and party napkins give them a drawer. If you have more then will fit in a drawer store them in a bin.

TOSS

No-brainer toss list: Vases you no longer love, platters that have seen better days, napkins and tablecloths you never use, and candles that are melted out of shape.

16.

Family Room and Living Room

341. Before you begin organizing, take a moment to think about how you want the room to function. You'll want to divide the room into activity zones, for watching television, reading, kid's play zone, exercise, game playing, entertaining, listening to music, piano playing, fireplace watching, and any other common activity. This way you can keep what you need near where you will be using it.

BONUS TIP:
Think about separating two competing activities into different rooms. For example, will someone need to practice his or her musical instrument when someone else will be trying to watch television?

342. Mounting your television on a wall bracket gets you back a large area of your room.

343. While not in use tuck your television away in an entertainment armoire. Many versions also offer ample storage space for DVDs, music, and more.

344. CDs and DVDs can be stored in a pop-up case. Pop-up cases are easy to use—just remove the CD or DVD from its original jewel case and slide it into a numbered slot in the case. Write the title on the list and then whenever you want one, slide the lever to the number of your title, push the button, and out pops the selected disc.

345. Use cord bundlers to rein in unruly cords and wires. While bundling the cords take a moment to label what the cord is attached to, this takes the guesswork out of finding the right cord when you go to unplug it.

346. Designate one place as the home for all your remotes. A drawer or a small basket may be a good choice. A less traditional storage option is to place Velcro on the back of the remotes and place a strip of Velcro on the wall; you can then stick the remote to the wall behind the couch.

347. All the guest pillows, blankets, and sheets can be tucked away in a trunk or ottoman with storage inside. The trunk or ottoman can then be used as extra seating.

BONUS TIP:

If you have samples of soap and other little sample bottles of lotions and things, place them there for guests' use as well.

348. Use all the vertical space you have. Select bookshelves that extend the full length from the floor to the ceiling.

349. Always have access to your outlets. Plug in a flat extension cord before you back a piece of furniture up against the outlet. You can then fit the item flush to the wall because the plug will not stick out.

350. Create an art wall to keep your walls from becoming cluttered with artwork. Choose one wall as the focal point and group selected artwork there.

351. Hang photographs on the wall to avoid tabletops from becoming cluttered with photo frames.

352. Before hanging up artwork or photographs cut a rough template of the sizes of the frames. Then place the templates on the wall to adjust the arrangement before nailing into the wall.

353. Traditional coffee and end tables lack a tremendous amount of functionality. Instead, opt for tables with multiple drawers or baskets underneath. This allows you to maximize the space.

354. Another creative storage solution for the living space is to substitute a trunk for your coffee table; it offers a large amount of storage in addition to making a distinct statement. An ottoman with storage inside and a tray on top makes a table when needed and extra seating at other times. A small chest of drawers works well as an end table.

355. Instead of buying new you can modify an existing coffee table or end table to make it more functional. Place a basket, container, or rolling bin beneath the table to make use of the previously wasted space.

356. Store photo albums on the bookshelf. Photo boxes fit well there too.

357. Place your current reading material including the TV programming guide in a small basket near the couch.

358. Store books by category to make them easy to locate on the shelf. Before you begin shelving the books, try to cut your book collection in half.

359. Too many books to fit on the shelves? If so, box some up, label them, and store them away. Then in six months, you can rotate the books and have a new collection.

BONUS TIP:

Make a note in your calendar to remind yourself when you want to rotate the books.

360. Be sure your books are returned by sticking one of your address labels inside the cover of a book before you lend it out. Track the books you have lent by holding onto the book jacket for hardcover books and keep a running list on the bookshelf for the softcover books.

361. Make gathering wood for the fireplace easy by lining a bucket or wood holder with a leather mat that has handles. Then when you need more wood instead of bringing it in piece by piece you can fill the mat and carry that.

BONUS TIP:

Even if you have young children you can still use your fireplace by adding a specially designed child gate.

362. Throw blankets work well tossed over the back of the couch. But if you prefer a cleaner look then simply toss them into an ottoman with a lid that doubles as storage.

TOSS

No-brainer toss list: Broken CD jewel cases, duplicate movies, photo frames you do not love, and exercise equipment you haven't used in six months or more.

17.
Playroom

363. Post rules for the playroom immediately. Some possible rules might include: only two toys out at a time, clean up before leaving the playroom, play dates help clean up ten minutes before they go home, etc.

BONUS TIP:
To get more cooperation, hold a short family meeting to get ideas for rules, vote on them, and post them.

364. Give everyone a ten-minute warning to tidy up before playtime ends. Anything not cleaned up when the bell goes off is put in an unclaimed bin. To get a toy out of the unclaimed bin you must help with a chore. And anything left in the unclaimed bin for over a month goes to charity.

365. Store items that need to be used with supervision up high or in a locked cabinet. This requires the children to ask you to get it down and you can keep a watchful eye.

366. Have the children help label the bins and containers. Each label can have the name and then a picture of what is inside.

367. Some children respond well to color-coding. You can store the arts and craft supplies in red bins, board games and puzzles in blue bins, cars and other vehicles in green bins, and so on.

368. To make toys and books new again, store some away. Then in a few months, rotate the ones from storage.

BONUS TIP:
To help you remember to rotate make a note on your calendar.

369. Children usually have a difficult time with lids. Do not use lids on bins or tubs that they use often.

370. Never lose a library book again. Designate one shelf or basket for borrowed items.

371. Place all the stuffed animals in a net and hang them up.

372. Help children learn how to share their belongings with others who have less. Ask each child to find one game, two stuffed animals, and one other item to give away. Be specific—it is too hard for them to just find "stuff to give away."

373. If a game has a missing piece and cannot be played without it then toss the game. If you want you can have one holding shelf for toys with missing pieces. If the piece is not found in a reasonable amount of time you let it go.

374. If you decide to toss games with missing pieces, then there is no need to keep the loose pieces themselves. But if you have a waiting time before you toss the game, then designate one basket for all the missing items. Anything unknown goes in the basket and if something is missing, you look there.

375. Keep puzzles and all their pieces together by color-coding them. Use different-colored markers and place a dot on the back of each piece and then the board itself.

376. Take board games out of their boxes. The boxes tend to break and it can be difficult to fit the pieces back in the box. Stack all the boards side by side in a bin and place the pieces for each one in a large Ziploc bag.

BONUS TIP:
The easiest way to label each bag of pieces is to cut the picture out of the box and pop in the instructions as well.

377. Toy boxes are usually deep, without dividers and poorly lit, making it easy to lose toys in the bottom. Opt for alternate storage and do not use a toy box. If you want to use a toy box do so only for one sort of toy such as stuffed animals.

378. Create a parking garage for large ride-on toys if they are used inside.

379. Hang a plastic over-the-door shoe holder on the back of the playroom door. It makes a great home for items like action figures and doll shoes. Place a second one lower for all the items that are okay for little hands to be able to reach without supervision.

380. Opt for shallow bins instead of deeper bins for storage. It makes it much easier to find things and they are not too heavy to move.

381. Rolling bins are a great option. They allow the children to roll toys over to where they want to play. It also makes clean up a snap since the container is right next to the play area.

382. Group arts and crafts by activity. One bin for washable painting with watercolors and brushes, another bin for finger paint and paints to be used under supervision. In another bin put crafty things, like glue, goggle eyes, scissors, and other craft supplies.

383. For specific projects, store all the pieces in a Ziploc bag.

384. Group coloring books in magazine holders by activity and age.

TOSS

No-brainer toss list: Broken toys, happy meal toys, paint that is almost used up, crayons bits, ripped books, and used coloring books.

18.

Bedrooms

385. Steer away from buying single articles of clothing with the hope of finding a matching piece. It is very difficult to match colors and fabrics. So, even if you buy the item from the sale rack, it is no bargain if it sits unused.

386. You do not have to use a dresser. Dressers tend to be challenging to store clothes in. When you stack items in a drawer they wrinkle and it is difficult to see what you own. In addition, they tend to collect all sorts of stuff on the top surface. A fantastic alternative is to use shelves or cubbies in the closet.

BONUS TIP:
Use the dresser in another area of the home. They work well as a sideboard in the dining room.

387. Use the space under the bed. Try to store covered items since it can be dusty down there.

BONUS TIP:
If your bed is too close to the floor to use the space underneath, then simply add bed risers.

388. Dresser mirrors only allow you to see half the picture. Instead, place a full-length mirror on the back of the bedroom or closet door.

389. Try giving each family member his or her own laundry basket. They get the basket to the washer on laundry day and then the basket is returned to them with fresh clothing that they can then put away.

390. To avoid having the corners of the room become dumping grounds, place something decorative there, like a table with a vase or something else that fits your décor.

391. If you tend to wear the same few outfits repeatedly because you forget what you own, then you might try creating a catalog. Lay out each outfit or article of clothing and take a photo of it. Then place the photos in a book to create your own catalog to flip through.

392. Space bags are not usually a helpful solution. Plus you have to be careful, since many times items stored in the bags come out with a chemical smell that does not wash out.

393. Accessory scarves hang well on a scarf hanger, which is a plastic hanger with holes in it that allows you room to pull one scarf through each hole. If you prefer to store the scarves lying flat then slip them into under-the-shelf baskets.

394. As you weed through the clothing, make a list of the items you want to replace. Then you can let go of some of the ones you have and look forward to shopping for articles of clothing you actually need.

395. A great way to keep nightstands clear is to have a small basket or container where you can place items to keep them out of sight. Then the nightstand can just hold the essentials.

BONUS TIP:
Reconsider how much reading material you want to store bedside. If you do not typically read in bed then move the reading pile to another room. Waking up to a pile of unfinished books and magazines is stressful.

396. To make cleaning the top of the nightstand a breeze, place your alarm clock and other essential items on a shallow tray. Then you simply need to lift the tray instead of each individual item to clean.

397. To keep your bedroom a restful and relaxing sanctuary, opt not to have a home office area in the room. Also do not keep paperwork or bills in the bedroom.

398. When sorting through your wardrobe ask yourself, "Would I buy this today if I were out shopping?" If the answer is yes then consider keeping it. But if the answer is no then realize the time has passed and you can now part with the article. If it is a meaningful article of clothing then toss it in your memory box.

399. Hooks—they're not just for kids. Hooks are perfect for holding a variety items. Place some hooks on the inside of the door as well as inside the closet. You can hang hats, umbrellas, tote bags, and more.

400. If you have a television in the bedroom a great way to hide it is by placing it in an armoire. That way you can stash all the accessories and media paraphernalia behind closed doors as well.

401. If there are a few pieces of jewelry you wear every day, instead of placing the items in a jewelry box, simply place them in a bowl or on a tray. That way they will be right there the next time you get ready.

402. Purses can be stored in a canvas purse organizer that hangs from a rod in a closet or you can attach to a wall. The other option is to line them up on a shelf, using shelf dividers so they do not tip over.

403. Another part of self-management is getting a handle on the clutter in your wallet or purse. It's common for people to carry business cards in their wallets. They take up a lot of space and are unnecessary. Take all the business cards out of your wallet daily and enter the contact information into your contact database. Get into a habit of emptying your wallet or purse every time you come home. It will only take a few minutes. This is much easier than having to spend hours sorting through papers whenever you get around to it.

404. Carry only the essentials in your purse. For a day or two, notice what you really use. What are you carrying around that you don't use? Also, look at the credit and other cards that you carry. Do you have more than one credit card? Do you stuff your wallet with tons of family pictures? An overabundance of makeup? Consider carrying cash, one credit card, your insurance card, and your auto club card in your wallet. Use a separate small photo album for a few recent family photos and a single key ring for all store discount key tags.

405. There is such a thing as too many organizing options. To avoid losing things in the pockets and slots of a tote bag or purse, assign a purpose to each pocket and slot. One for the cell phone, one for pen and paper, one for sunglasses, and so on. After a few days of being consistent and using each pocket only for its purpose you'll be able to find everything quickly.

406. Carry a Ziploc bag in your purse where you can place garbage. This makes for a very easy clean out.

407. Make switching bags and purses easy. Store your items in smaller bags. Makeup in a makeup bag. Odds and ends in another zipper pouch. Sunglasses, and other essentials in another small bag. This way you can pull out the bags and toss them into another purse instead of moving each individual item.

408. Keep the bedroom tidy with new rules; for example, in our home, the last one out of bed makes the bed.

409. Make chores easy; keep the supplies in the room where you will need them. Store the sheet sets for the bed in the room along with cleaning supplies.

DOUBLE BONUS TIP:

Trunks and covered baskets make a great decorative storage option for these items. Try storing sheets laying flat under the mattress; they will be wrinkle free when you go to put them on.

410. Keep a large garbage can in the bedroom. For easy use, consider not using the lid.

BONUS TIP:

If you have a walk-in closet keep a garbage can there to collect tags, dry cleaning bags, and other trash.

TOSS

No-brainer toss list: Clothing you can donate, furniture that no longer works for you in the room, reading material that has stacked up, and sheet sets for mattress sizes you no longer own. Send items to the dry cleaner if they need it, including mending if you haven't gotten to it yet.

19.

Kid's Bedrooms

411. To keep artwork from decorating every inch of your kitchen cabinet space you might try setting up an art gallery. A wall in the playroom, a corner of the family room, or an alcove in the child's room will work well. Have them place their newest and best creations in the gallery. Older work can be added to the memory box (two pieces a month is a good rule), passed along to family members, used as backgrounds in photo albums, or used to wrap gifts with.

412. Older artwork can be retired from the gallery and stored in a clean pizza box, the perfect size for all the oversized creations.

413. To help children remember what they are responsible for, post simple checklists. A checklist in the bathroom can remind them to brush their teeth and wash their hands. A checklist near their closet can help them remember to pack what they need for school, like gym clothes, musical instrument, scouting uniforms, etc.

414. A toy hammock can be a perfect solution to get all the stuffed animals up and off the floor. Hang the hammock in one corner of the room for easy clean up.

BONUS TIP:

When hanging the hammock, remember that it will sag under the weight of the toys, so hang it up higher than where you want it to finally rest.

415. Don't forget to use the back of the door. Hang a plastic shoe caddy low enough for children to reach. Then store all sorts of stuff inside remembering to make each pocket for one category. You can even label the pockets. Toys with little pieces work well here.

416. Stop nagging the children to clean up. Give them each a tote bag and when you need them to pick up their room hang the tote bag on the bedroom doorknob. Then the child can grab the bag, fill it up, and distribute the toys where they belong.

417. Prefill a small tote bag with portable games. Grab that bag anytime you might need to keep little ones occupied, like when going on a long car ride or out to dinner.

418. Pack a duffle bag with all the things needed for a sleepover. Then the next time there is a slumber party, a sleepover, or an overnight trip you can grab the bag on the go.

419. Ziploc bags are the perfect way to contain small parts: to games, puzzle pieces, doll accessories and so many other little things.

420. Tuck pajamas under the pillow or slip them inside a pillowcase so you can always find them at bedtime.

421. Pop up toy bins are a great option for larger toys such as stuffed animals and indoor balls.

422. Shoe racks can be a challenge for little ones to use. Instead, toss everyday shoes in a laundry basket and place fancier shoes on a shelf.

423. Sleeping bags can be stuffed in a flat bin and rolled under the bed—a good use of the often-wasted space under the bed.

424. Sporting equipment is best kept in the garage or a shed. However, the accessories, such as soccer socks, karate uniforms, and other items needed in the bedroom should be stored separately from every day clothing.

425. For little girls a vanity can be a great place to tuck away hair accessories. A simple slender table, mirror, and stool will work just fine. On the table, place a few fun baskets as storage units.

426. Schedule time for the kids to tidy up their rooms. Just like school, home-work, practice, and planned birthday parties, you also need to plan for clutter-clearing and cleaning up. It will not happen in spare time. You can make the time fun by playing music, setting a timer and trying to beat the clock, or having a fun treat after-wards.

TOSS

No-brainer toss list: Broken toys, ripped books, outgrown toys, toys with missing pieces, dangerous toys, and stuffed animals with no hope of cleaning.

20.

Bathrooms

427. Hang a clock in every bathroom to keep you on time when you are on a schedule.

428. An over-the-door metal basket organizer meant for the pantry works wonders in the bathroom. There are a variety of adjustable baskets, which allow you to store a bunch of stuff. Your scale, spare rolls of toilet paper, tub toys, shower caps, and more.

429. You can place all the bottles of hair care products in a basket under the sink, in a drawer, in the medicine cabinet, or line them up on a tray on the vanity.

430. Store your makeup in groups. Separate your day makeup from your evening makeup. That way you won't have to dig around through a bunch of pieces to find what you need.

431. A cutlery tray placed in a drawer works well for cosmetics.

432. If you tend to have a variety of sample sizes of makeup then place them in their own basket. And if you have lots, then group them by category and store them in baskets. Do not keep products that you would never use, and be sure to watch the expiration dates.

433. Other sample sizes of products can be stored in a basket and put out for guests.

434. Install a second toilet paper roll holder so you'll only have to change the paper half as often.

BONUS TIP:

If you have children or pets who find it fun to unroll the toilet paper you can purchase a safety lock to stop that from happening.

435. If you complete a task outside the bathroom, such as combing a child's hair in the living room, then store the necessary items in the living room instead of carrying them from one room to another all the time.

436. Scrunchies can live on the cardboard tube from the center of a roll of paper towels. When they're spread out like that, you'll be able to see what you own and pick the one you want to use.

437. Barrettes work well clipped to a wide decorative strand of ribbon.

438. A cupcake tin works well for storing barrettes and scrunchies. Toss in one type per cup and you will always be able to find the one you are looking for.

439. Medicine cabinets work best when they are not crammed full. Give each shelf a purpose. Maybe one for razors, one for toothpaste, one for deodorant, and one for jars of cream.

440. To maximize the space in the medicine cabinet, consider slipping on under-the-shelf organizers. You can add one for the tube of toothpaste, one for the razor, and even one for toothbrushes.

441. Suction cup holders are an easy way to store things. The newer type has a vacuum lock so they do not fall off like the older types. They are specifically designed to hold a variety of products, razors, toothbrushes (even the ones with the oversized handles), and more.

442. Also on the market are suction cup baskets. One stuck to the wall makes a perfect home for commonly used items like hairbrushes or men's shavers.

443. Utilize the space on the inside of the cabinet doors. Install an organizer for a hairdryer and curling iron or something else you need a storage place for.

444. Bath salts, body scrubs, and other spa products are best stored in their own bin or basket. Some are decorative enough that you might keep a basket out as part of the décor.

445. Tweezers and other grooming instruments can be stored in a shallow tray in a drawer.

446. Commonly used items such as tissues, cotton swabs stored in a mug, and other items can be placed on a tray. Then for cleaning you only have to lift up the tray rather than moving all the items individually.

447. Create a nail care caddy for all the supplies needed for a manicure. Having one container to tote around is much easier than looking all over for the individual items.

448. If you carry polishes to a nail salon to have your nails painted with the colors you own (a smart tip so you can touch up your own nails) then create a salon bag with the items you take with you. Include flip flops for a pedicure, polishes, and small bills for tips.

449. Create two first aid kits. One for minor cuts that you can grab what you need easily and one for major injury. Take one small plastic bin or basket and fill it with Band-Aids and antibiotic ointment. Then take a larger container and fill it with the ice packs, splints, ace bandages, large gauze pads, and other first aid necessities. Label each container and store them away.

450. Store medications by category and person. Use a few small containers and separate the medications. Allergy medications might be one category, cold and flu another. Anything for children can go in a bin of its own. Label each container and store them on a shelf.

BONUS TIP:

If you have pet medications store them in their own container and away from the medications meant for people.

451. Tub toys can be stored in a tub toy holder that hangs from the shower rod on the outside of the shower. Another way is to use a plastic container and when bath time is done simply toss them in. An alternative is to install a spring loaded pole with baskets in the shower. Give the toys one or two baskets to live in.

452. To keep your bar soap from leaving soap scum on the shower walls, suction cup a soap saver to the wall, away from the spray of the water. This is a plastic cup with drainage holes that fits a bar of soap. This will also help make the soap last longer.

453. To get rid of all the bottles cluttering up your shower, hang a dispenser inside the shower. Fill each section with a shampoo, body wash, or other containers. They come in many sizes with two to eight sections.

454. Another way to eliminate clutter in the shower is to give everyone in the house a shower caddy. A simple plastic container with drainage holes and a handle, similar to the ones college students use to take shower supplies with them to the bathroom from their dorm room. The caddy can hold hair care products, soap, face care products, loofah sponges, pumice stones, and much more. After a shower, the caddy can be stowed away on a shelf in the bathroom or linen closet nearby.

455. Label the shelves of the bathroom closet and the drawers. This makes it easy to find what you are looking for and you can easily put things where they belong. Plus, it is simple to see what you are out of when making a shopping list.

BONUS TIP:

If you don't like the look of a label on the outside of a drawer, place the label on the edge of the drawer so it only shows when you pull it out.

456. Store spare towels in the bathroom. Short on space? Here are some creative storage options. Roll the towels so you can fit more on the shelf. Store rolled towels in a wall-mounted towel rack or a wine rack. You can also purchase a towel stand, which fits about ten folded towels, or stand rolled towels on end in a basket.

457. If you need a step stool for a child consider leaving it out. There is no sense putting it away if it is used often.

458. If you own a pedestal sink, you can create extra storage by skirting the sink with a coordinating fabric. A perfect way to disguise your storage space.

459. If you have a traditional vanity then some of the underneath storage is lost to the pipes. To maximize the space, use a slat shelf that adjusts to fit around your pipes.

460. Because the space under a sink is usually dark and deep, you might consider installing a slide out shelf or basket, which are inexpensive and easy to install.

461. To increase the amount of storage space in the bathroom you can hang wall shelves and organizers or put in an over-the-toilet shelving unit. This would be the ideal place to store spare toilet paper, feminine hygiene products, first aid kits, cleaning supplies, and more.

462. A convenient way to keep bottles of things like mouthwash handy is to fill smaller bottles that are more decorative and keep them on the vanity. Then keep the oversized bottles in a nearby closet for refilling.

463. A decorative way to store spare rolls of toilet paper is to place them in a basket with a few rolled up towels. An alternative is to use a toilet paper stand.

464. Sit a garbage can in the bathroom, place spare liners in the bottom, line the can, and remove the lid. Not having a lid on it makes it much more user friendly and there is less to clean since there is no lid to get dirty.

465. A small magazine rack or a reading rack hung from the toilet tank is a great way to store reading material out of the way.

466. If you prefer not to carry caddies in and out of the bathroom, hang an over-the-door rack and designate one basket per person to fill with all their items.

467. If you have children, create a separate container with children's Band-Aids so you don't end up with a cartoon character Band-Aid on at work.

468. Stick a few utility hooks on the back of the bathroom door at varying heights. Then hang bathrobes and wet towels on them when not in use. Command hooks by 3M are a great choice. They are inexpensive, repositionable, and do not mar surfaces.

469. Put little gift or freebie bath products for guests in a basket on top of the toilet tank or in a gift bag on their pillow.

TOSS

No-brainer toss list: Expired medications, old toothbrushes, mildewed tub toys, outdated reading material, old product samples, makeup in colors you don't wear, and bottles with too little left in them to save.

JUNK ROOM

This is the room where you put things when you don't know where else they should go. So you put them there "just for now" and before you know it the entire room is filled with "junk." You know the room—the one where you open the door, toss something else in, pull the door shut quickly, and run away. But you may have dreams of using the space as a guest bedroom, an office, a craft room, or some other functional room. Instead, it is wasted space and a place that may cause you embarrassment or stress. The best way to conquer this room is to start small. It is virtually impossible to clear the entire room at once, so set your timer for eighteen minutes, and go in. Focus on one area; it might be the spot when you first walk in or the space with the least amount of stuff. As the timer ticks down follow the three steps: first sorting like with like, that is the part that takes the longest. Once you can see what you have you can put away what you use and love, giving the items you no longer want to a local charity. After that maintain your newly unearthed room by promising yourself not to place anything there if it does not belong.

21.

Laundry and Utility Rooms

470. To keep all your laundry stuff organized and out of sight, especially in a small area, use an armoire. Place a laundry sorter in the lower section where dirty laundry can be tossed. Detergents and bleach can be stored on the shelf and a basket can hold all the stain removers. On the inside of the doors, you can hang a towel bar for rags, a lint roller, and a sewing kit for mending. You can also stick up a stain removal chart and directions on how to run the washer and dryer. The best part is that you can use the slide out shelf as your folding space and ironing board as long as you cover it with a heat resistant material first.

471. Laundry butlers are organizers specially made to fit between the washing machine and dryer—no more clothes falling between the two machines.

472. Keep ironing boards out of site by opting for the hanging version. The ironing board will hang by hooks over the door. You can either fold it down for use or just store it there and take it down when you need it. Some versions also hold the iron itself.

473. Keep a stash of hangers near the dryer to make it easy to hang up clothing as the items come out of the dryer.

474. Hang brooms and mops from a broom handle holder where each handle pops into a spring-loaded spot.

475. Keep a cleaning caddy handy for quick cleanups. For example, a drip of detergent is much easier to clean up before it dries.

476. Use a folding table if you lack a space to fold laundry, or if the space originally meant for folding laundry is now overflowing with other stuff. A table with fold down sides will take up less space. Plus, if you fold the sides down when you are done it cannot be a catchall for other stuff.

477. Gain more time by folding less. Reconsider what you spend your time folding. Do undergarments really need to have perfect creases in them? Can you roll the towels instead of folding them?

478. If you currently have a backlog of laundry, consider dropping it off at a wash by the pound laundromat so they can do a few loads to get you caught up.

BONUS TIP:
This also works well when you return from a vacation to keep you from becoming backlogged.

479. An old toothbrush is a perfect tool for scrubbing out laundry stains. Keep a few handy in your stain kit. Also in your stain kit keep baby wipes, which get out an amazing number of stains, hairspray for ink marks, and other stain-treating products. Posting a stain guide nearby is helpful for easy reference.

480. Keep a dishpan nearby so you can soak items that need it. This is especially helpful when you have limited time but want to keep a stained item wet so the stain does not set.

481. Keep a container nearby to collect lose money and other items that come out of pockets before the clothing is laundered.

482. Help others pitch in: post easy to follow directions by the washer and dryer so everyone in the house can run a load of laundry.

483. A laundry sorter is a perfect way to take one step out of the laundry process. Instead of having everyone lump their dirty clothes in one basket or hamper, have them sort them. Place a laundry sorter near where clothing is taken off, or in the laundry room. When clothes are placed there to be washed they can go into one of three bins: whites, lights, and darks. Each section holds up to two loads of laundry so there is plenty of room for all the clothes, and then you don't have to spend any time sorting...

484. Make a new family rule: in our home, laundry can only be placed in the hamper if it is turned right side out, zippers are zipped, buttons are buttoned, and the pockets are empty.

485. Keep a cup in the powder detergent for easy measuring.

BONUS TIP:

If you shop at warehouse stores and have an over-sized container of detergent then spend a few minutes and make small packets of it for individual washes. Pour liquid detergent into old plastic containers or powdered detergent into Ziploc bags. This is also helpful if other family members are pitching in to help with the laundry—no measuring required.

486. Keep one unmatched sock container. Make it a game to go through the mismatches. Set a timer and see how many matches you can make before it goes off. Or make it a matching game with children. One final way is to delegate it out as one of the household chores up for grabs.

487. Prevent the unmatched socks from piling up by keeping them paired together through the wash. You can toss mated socks into a mesh lingerie bag, and then you know the mates are together. Another option is a product called the sock pro. They are small plastic disks; you simply slip one pair through the disk and then launder as usual. One other option is to use a laundry marker to place colored dots on the bottoms of socks. Use one color marker for each person in the house, then the matching will be narrowed down. Lastly, if you just wear all-of-a-kind socks they will all match each other.

488. Keep a small pile of the items in need of repair. The pile is best kept in a portable container. That way you can carry it to another room when you make time to do the mending, like while watching a movie. In your mending basket, you can also stock a small sewing kit so you'll have everything you need on hand.

BONUS TIP:

Also store a mini can of hairspray in your kit, a little on the end of a piece of thread makes threading a needle a breeze and keeping a magnet in the kit makes it easy to attract and store pins and needles.

489. If you are starting out with a large pile of mending you can catch up quickly by sending it out to a tailor. That way you'll be starting from scratch. But before you spend any time or money on the mending ask yourself, "If it has sat here this long do I really need it?"

490. Short on space for a drying rack? Try one that attaches to the wall or hangs on the back of the door and pulls out for use.

491. Set a timer to ring as a reminder when the washer or dryer is finished. It keeps you on track and stops clothes from wrinkling in the dryer.

492. Be sure to have a wastebasket handy in the laundry room.

493. Make the laundry room a fun place to spend time. Play music, paint it a bright color, or add fun artwork and photographs to the walls.

494. Set guidelines for what is actually dirty. How long are towels, sheets, and clothing used before they are considered dirty? Make it a household rule that the way to get clothing ironed is not to put it back into the laundry hamper to be rewashed. Instead, use the iron or hang it in a steamy shower. And if clean clothing gets mixed with dirty laundry because clean clothing was left in the laundry basket instead of being put away, it does not mean you can simply put it all back in the wash to be rewashed. Try to separate it out and keep clean clothes out of the laundry basket.

495. Be sure to wash lint givers such as throw rugs and chenille sweaters separate from lint takers like black pants, fleece, and velour.

496. You can attach a net to the inside of the dryer door to hold items such as sneakers while they are drying.

TOSS

No-brainer toss list: Empty detergent bottles, expired stain sticks, nests of hangers, unknown items that came out of pockets a long time ago.

22.

Workshop and Tool Area

497. Hanging an over-the-door shoe cubby on the door or the wall offers a bunch of storage for tools and other supplies.

498. Remember to keep like items with like. Store all project scraps in one place, all the tools in another, and so on.

499. Hang old kitchen cabinets for tons of extra storage. If you don't have old cabinets of your own to hang, find someone who is remodeling their kitchen or take a look around during cleanup week.

500. Be sure you have a large garbage can nearby and leave the lid off for easy access.

501. Rent rarely used or expensive pieces of equipment such as a snowblowers or extension ladders instead of buying them. If you prefer to own the item instead of renting it then see whom else you know who might want the same machine. Then you can pool your money, buy one, and take turns storing it.

502. Tools can be tossed in a milk crate or a bucket for storage.

503. Use a piece of scrap wood to store screwdrivers and other similar tools. Simply drill holes in a variety of diameters in the wood and mount it to the wall. Then slip the tool in the hole for easy storage.

504. If you need to store sand, kitty litter, or salt for melting snow in the winter months, place open bags in milk crates so they remain upright and do not tip, spilling the contents. An alternative is to use a funnel and pour some into a few empty milk containers, be sure to label them clearly. Storing it this way will make it easy to pour the salt or sand as needed.

505. A spice rack can be a good place to store screws and nails. Place only one kind per bottle and then place the bottles in the rack.

506. Another way to store nails and other little items is to use jars. Nail the lid of the jar to a beam above the workstation and then screw the jar on and off as needed.

507. Keep small miscellaneous items accessible by hanging a magnetic strip near the workstation. Then use magnetic jars with clear lids to store the items in. Then they will be at your fingertips.

508. Tackle boxes can be the perfect solution for where to store small odds and ends such as nuts, bolts, and screws.

509. Mount a magnetized sheet of metal to the wall. There you can store drill bits, nails, and other magnetized items.

510. Toss all broken items. Keep a running list of items to replace.

511. To keep projects from ending up on the back burner, schedule time for them on the calendar. If it is a large project then break it up into smaller tasks to keep the momentum going. If you are not ready to place the project on the calendar then let the supplies for the project go to someone who is ready right now to do the project.

512. Using a slat wall or a pegboard is a great way to keep things up and off the workspace. Slat walls allow you to slip specially designed organizers to hold items. Pegboards also work well and work best when you outline the item that belongs there, so you can replace it easily.

513. An old chest of drawers works well as a storage unit. And if you are going to place a storage cabinet in the space consider getting one that is thirty-two to thirty-six inches tall, that way it will double as a work surface. If the piece is not that tall then prop it up on cinder blocks or wood to reach the desired height.

514. Hang a fire extinguisher by the door in the work area. Be sure to notify your insurance company—many will offer a discount on premiums for this safety measure.

515. Use a three-ring binder filled with sheet protectors to store warranties and manuals for the machines and equipment. You can even keep order forms for replacement parts and part numbers in the binder. Label it "workshop" and stand it on a shelf for easy access.

516. A funnel nailed to the wall can work for holding cords and wires. Place them in, pull one end through the funnel and then they won't tangle.

517. Keep spare parts and extras organized—like spare screws for a bookshelf and doorknobs—by placing each in a Ziploc bag. Be sure to label the bag and if there is an instruction manual or assembly directions place it in the bag as well.

TOSS

No-brainer toss list: Rusted equipment, nails and screws you'll never need, and bits of wood you won't use.

23.
Gardening Center

518. Lack space for all your garden supplies? Use an armoire. With drawers on the bottom half you can tuck all sorts of goodies inside. In the upper cabinet portion, screw a pegboard against the back wall to hang all your tools and a roll of paper towels. Shelves work well to store pots and other supplies. You can hang even more tools on the inside of the cabinet doors. Line the shelves and work surface with a washable contact paper for easy clean up.

519. Organize your tools by task—plant, weed, water, and reap. Remember the rule to keep like with like.

520. Install a pegboard on one or more walls of the garage. Then you can hang your tools for easy reach.

521. A slat wall can also be installed on a wall. Baskets and containers designed specifically for gardening items slip into the slats on the wall.

522. If your water hose does not have a wheel to wrap it up with then consider buying one. These allow you to wind up the hose and store it tangle-free.

523. Flat hoses are a good option because they are easy to store. The down side is that you have to unroll the entire hose for it to work; you cannot just turn it on for a quick watering.

524. Paint the handles of your tools a bright color so you don't lose them in the grass.

525. An old golf bag or a large garbage can on wheels make a perfect home for rakes and other taller tools.

526. Accessories like stakes, wire, and fencing can be kept in a bucket. That way you can easily see what you have and you will be less likely to rebuy something you already own.

527. Garden decorations are only useful if you can find the ones you have when you want to use them. Keep them easy to see by storing them in clear containers that you label.

528. Store seed packets by category—fruit, vegetables, perennials, annuals, and so on. Slip each category into a clear plastic bin and label it clearly. Remember that they typically have expiration dates on them, so store only what you truly intend to use.

529. Buckets and tote bags are a great way to store tools, hats, gloves, shoes, knee protectors, and other gardening accessories. They make it easy to carry them out to the garden.

530. Keep deer from eating your plants by hanging CDs or foil pie plates around the garden. The reflection startles them and keeps them from coming close enough to make a meal of your garden.

531. A top loading dispenser works well for potting soil. It fills from the top and has a small door towards the bottom that opens so you can dispense as much or as little as you would like.

532. Nest pots inside one another and stack trays by size. Be realistic and keep only the best pots in a few sizes that you may truly need.

533. Place water level detectors in the pots of your indoor plants. They change color to indicate when you need to add water.

534. A rolling cart filled with potting supplies works well as a movable workstation. You can roll the cart out when you want to work and put it back when you are done.

535. For a fixed workstation, you might consider a wood board with a hole towards one side. Then once you are done working you can push the dirt and waste to the hole and have it dump into a waste container below for easy clean up.

TOSS

No brainer toss list: Seed packets for flowers or vegetables you do not grow or that are past their expiration date, outdated fertilizer, old watering cans, broken or rusted tools, gardening gloves without a mate, and hoses that have holes.

24.
Craft Area

536. No craft room? No problem. Use an armoire. A slide out shelf will make a perfect work surface. You can screw hooks into the inside of the doors and hang scissors. Put in a lamp for task lighting. You can even set your sewing machine on the shelf. A garbage can and storage shelves round out the space.

537. Sliding spools of ribbon onto a dowel or thin curtain rod hung near the craft table allows you to use what you need easily.

BONUS TIP:
This also works well for gift wrapping ribbons.

538. An alternative to using the rod for ribbons is to place each ribbon in a funnel and pull the end through the bottom of the funnel to avoid tangling.

539. Purchase magazine holders from an office supply store to keep books, instructions, and patterns organized. Keep only what you will actually use and label them for easy reference. Craft and hobby magazines can also be easily organized using the magazine holders. Label the outside of the holder and slip in the editions you want to save.

540. Tackle boxes work well for sorting and storing little items like beads, gemstones, and embellishments.

541. Wine racks work well for storing rolls of fabric. You can easily see what you have and it is a snap to get to.

542. Another way to store fabric is by hanging it over hangers in a closet or on a pants trolley.

543. Before storing fabrics in a box, attach a fabric swatch to the outside so you can easily see what is inside without opening the box each time.

544. Tall cans, like the tall thin ones used for some potato chip containers hold paintbrushes (brush side up) and some of the other taller crafting tools.

BONUS TIP:
If you have a lot of one kind, try a few containers labeled for each category.

545. If your craft area is short on space, try storing the craft books on a bookshelf in another room.

BONUS TIP:
If you have a friend or family member who often buys the same craft books you do, buy one, and share it. Or borrow them from the library.

546. A great way to collect all the ideas of things you might like to do in the future is to use an accordion folder. Label each tab with a category and you can slip the idea into its section for easy reference in the future.

547. Organizing all the undone projects starts with a realistic look at them. If you haven't finished them yet, are you really going to? It is ok if you choose not to; you can simply pass them along to someone who will. For all the undone ones you truly do plan to complete, place them in a container, label it clearly, and store them away. Then before you shop for another project, look through the ones you already own.

BONUS TIP:

Host a project swap party with friends, family, and neighbors. Have everyone bring the projects they are willing to give up, even if they are already started, and everyone can pick new projects.

548. A rolling cart works well to house project tools. The cart can be rolled to where you are working and then rolled away when not in use.

549. To ensure that you have time to actually work on your hobby you must schedule that time on your calendar. There will never be spare time during the week to work on a project; you must make the time.

550. To keep commonly used items, especially small ones, at your fingertips, hang a square of metal sheeting near your work area. Then place the items in magnetic jars that simply stick to the wall. Many come with clear tops so you can see what is inside at a glance. If not, glue one of the items on the outside of the lid so you can easily tell what is inside.

551. Spice racks are a perfect solution for glitter. Pour the glitter into the spice container and it will easily shake out the top. No more annoying spills.

552. Loose scraps of material and little miscellaneous items need a home too. Group the bits into categories and contain them together. Be sure to label the drawer or bin you put them into.

553. Use color-coded labels or color-coded box lids to keep different types of items for different projects. Get clear plastic boxes with different color lids; use the red for sewing, green for knitting, and so on. With the clear view, you'll be able to quickly see what's inside.

554. Dried flowers are best stored in holes drilled through a shelf or in tall cones nailed to the wall.

555. Oversized scrapbook paper can be sorted into twelve-by-twelve inch, plastic stacking trays. Other sizes fit in the standard stacking office trays. Literature sorters, sometimes called mail slots, are another option.

556. Utilize your wall space; put up shelving and label the shelves with the names of the different types of project materials you have. This makes it easier to put items away and you can easily tell what you are out of. Baskets also fit well on most shelving and they can keep items handy. In utilizing your wall space, there are organizers that you can purchase too; some are even made to house specialty craft items.

557. You can also install a pegboard and hang your tools on it for easy access. You might also trace around the tool, so when it is not in its place you will know it is missing.

558. A thread rack will keep your thread organized and easy to see and reach.

559. A corkboard at eye level to pin instructions or patterns makes reading them easy.

560. Skeins of yarn are best stored in small bins by color and texture. For example, "baby colors," "holiday," "black and white," and "odds and ends" of yarn.

561. If you are in the middle of a craft project such as knitting, you can place everything you need in a tote bag and carry it with you.

TOSS

No-brainer toss list: Paint and glue bottles with so little in them that they are not worth saving, instructions for projects you no longer own, books for projects you will never do, any broken tools, brushes that have lost bristles, anything that does not work well.

25.

Photographs

562. If you are like most people, you have a backlog of photos to sort and place in albums. The simplest thing to do is to start a new system today for all future photos and work on the backlog in small amounts. If you wait until you sort the backlog to do recent photos you will never catch up.

563. A great photo system for traditional prints is to choose decorative photo boxes, and label them by category or chronologically. Then as new rolls of film are developed, place the photos in the their proper box. These boxes are so decorative that you can leave them sitting out on a bookshelf.

564. To catch up on the backlog of photos, grab a handful at a time, maybe while watching a movie or chatting on the phone. Sort the handful into the prelabeled boxes and then do another handful the next day.

565. Currently on the market is a photo organizer that will hold over two thousand photos in an acid free, light resistant box. Write-on/wipe-off index tabs allow you to sort the photos at your leisure.

566. As you sort the photos, keep envelopes handy; you're bound to come across duplicates which you can place directly in the envelope and mail out to family and friends. Even if you do know their address off the top of your head, write their name on the envelope and fill in the rest later.

567. Give yourself permission not to scrapbook all your photos, as this would be more than a full-time job itself. Instead, if you have the desire to scrapbook, make the time and create smaller specially themed albums such as a trip to Disneyland or a good friend's wedding.

568. Once you have your photos in order avoid the backlog from happening again. Get in the habit of handling the photos the minute they come back from the developer. Also, be more selective when you're taking photos; rethink your decision to get doubles; don't let your undeveloped rolls of film pile up; and try mail-order processing.

569. And what about negatives? Keep the negatives to the most special photos only. Store them separate from the albums so that if anything ever destroys the albums, you'll be able to reproduce the photos. However, for the everyday shots it is easier to make a copy of the photo itself.

570. If storing negatives separately is too much trouble, you can also store them in an envelope you adhere to the inside of the photo album's back cover.

571. If you have gone digital then you may have a backlog of photos in the camera or on your computer desktop. Just like traditional photos, digital photos need to be categorized. After every use download the photos, keeping only the best of the best and place them into a folder with an easy reference name. "Picture 234293u3" is less helpful than "Thanksgiving 05 at Kristy's House."

572. Photo organizing does not need to be a chore. Host a photo party. Invite friends, family, and neighbors, and ask them to bring a bag of photos and an album or photo box. Then you can spend the time sharing memories while you each fill your own albums or boxes.

TOSS

No-brainer toss list: Toss any photo if you can't recognize the people in it, it is of the floor or ceiling, it is blurry, it is an unflattering shot, or if you have many that look similar. In addition, separate out all the duplicates to pass along to others.

26.

Car

573. Try this new house rule—in our family, no one eats in the car. It keeps a lot of the mess out of the car and forces you to sit and have meals instead of gulping as you drive.

574. Maintain the maintenance record. Toss a small spiral notebook into your glove compartment, and every time your car is serviced jot down the date and a quick note. You can leave the notebook in an envelope where you can place the maintenance receipts and warranties.

575. Get in the habit of filling the gas tank when it is half empty.

576. Tuck a few menus from your favorite restaurants in the glove compartment so that on a busy night you can call in an order for pick up or delivery.

577. Keep a folder with commonly used addresses, directions, and maps.

578. Keep a list of the hours of operation for the stores and places you go to most often.

579. Keep a clipboard in the car, with a pen attached to it and some sheets of notepaper. This way no time will be wasted; if you are waiting to pick someone up and they are late, you'll have paper to write down a shopping list or anything else.

580. Keep a list of commonly dialed numbers in the car. You can tape them to the back of the clipboard.

BONUS TIP:

Be sure to have a list of numbers needed in a emergency. That way if you get a flat tire on the way to pick up your child, you can call someone else to fill in for you.

581. Make it a habit to check the car's lights and wiper blades every time you adjust the clocks for daylight savings time.

BONUS TIP:
When you replace one blown out light bulb replace the other one as well. If they were installed around the same time, they've gotten about the same amount of use and the other one will blow soon.

582. Keep a gift bag, a few pieces of tissue paper, and a generic greeting card in the car. This way you can wrap a gift or write out a card on short notice.

583. Special car toys just for travel time work well to occupy the children.

584. CDs, DVDs, CD players, and all their cords, fit nicely into a back of the seat organizer. It simply hangs off the headrest and offers a bunch of pockets in a variety of sizes, sure to fit all the items. Back of the seat organizers are great to organize other items as well.

585. Old prescription bottles are a perfect size to hold coins for tolls and parking meters.

586. Try this new household rule—in our family, no one leaves anything in the car that does not belong there.

587. Leave some items you use all the time in the car. If dance lessons are a weekly event, you can leave the dance bag in the car.

588. If you want you can leave coupons and gift certificates in the car. That way you'll be sure to have them when you are at the store.

589. The underutilized glove box: Instead of stashing a car manual you use only once in awhile in it, place the manual in the trunk and utilize the space for more commonly needed items such as tissues, aspirin, deodorant, car registration and insurance card, breath freshener, pens and paper, cologne, a small flashlight, drinking straws, hand wipes, bank withdrawal/deposit slips, tire pressure gauge, small snacks, disposable camera (so in the event of an accident you can record damage and the position of the cars), and take out menus.

590. Keep paper towels, maps, and a small trashcan inside the car. Velcro strips will keep them from sliding around.

591. Inside the trunk, keep a supply of fresh water (change often), inflate-a-tire spray (caution: using the product renders the tire unusable—tire stores can not patch even a nail hole if this product is in the tire due to its flammable nature), extra paper towels, a paintbrush (to use after a trip to the beach to easily brush sand off your feet), towels for the beach or gym, large durable snacks, an emergency kit (including items like jumper cables, a large flashlight, a large "help" sign, flares, a first aid kit), comfortable change of clothes (old sneakers, socks, sweats, etc.) You can change from a nice suit to sweatpants to check under the hood. Or you could switch from high heels to sneakers so you can walk more easily for assistance.

592. If your child does eat in the car, place a towel under the child's car seat for easy clean up. It will catch all the crumbs and spills.

593. Cargo bins are a simple way to keep things from rolling around in your trunk. You can place bags in them as well as store items like your car manual and supplies. They come in two versions, "pop-up" and "strap-in."

TOSS

No-brainer toss list: Empty wrappers, old receipts, leftover snacks that need to be tossed, pens that do not work, loose change sitting around, and used napkins.

Part Eight:

Applying the Tips to Paper, the Office, and the Computer

Do you ever wonder if you are the only person in the world who has to move piles of paper off a surface to work or eat? Or if you are the only one who has lost an important paper in a stack of important papers? Do you ever think you might be keeping too much, but then wonder what you could get rid of? If you've ever cut out an article from the newspaper, clipped out a hairstyle you might like to try, or jotted down a website to check out, and then promptly lost it, don't despair, there is hope.

Our lives are filled with so much paper, I'd like to find the person who promised me a paperless society and give him or her a talking to. Paperless, ha! Besides all the paper you already have, more comes in the mail every day. It's enough to make you want to take down your mailbox or tape the mail slot shut.

Paper is by far the number one complaint when it comes to clutter. The good news (yes, there is good news) is that I have a no fail solution for all your paper. Are you a bit skeptical? I promise you that this solution works, even if you are one of those people who wants to have all your papers out so you don't forget about something. Because you know the old adage—out of sight out of mind. Well, not in this case. Ready? Let's get started before today's mail is delivered and even more paper comes into your life.

Here's a fair warning before we enter the paper zone: 97 percent of what is filed is never referenced again. That means aside from what you use and what you are required to keep for tax purposes, you need to be very discerning about what papers you spend your time organizing.

Remember it is easier to call a utility company and request a year to date statement if you want to know your usage instead of locating all the stubs and calculating it yourself.

27.

No Fail
Paper Solution

This is a foolproof system for dealing with all the pending papers in your life. This is the exact one I've used for years, and the one I set my clients up with. This is the real McCoy. Don't be fooled by imitations. Here is how to organize your papers the Jamie Novak way.

This system is good for all the pending papers in your life. You know, the ones that sit in piles on your tables and countertops waiting for you to do something with them. Or the ones you are leaving out so you do not forget about them. The trick is to keep them accessible without having them scattered every which way from Tuesday. You are going to do this by using a desktop file box. Keep this desktop box someplace easy to reach like on the kitchen countertop since you want to have the papers on hand.

This desktop box has no lid, but has sides and is about twelve inches deep, large enough to accommodate about twenty-five letter-size hanging folders. The boxes come in a wide variety of styles and colors and are available at office stores and most home goods stores, usually for under twenty dollars. See the reference section for a list of stores where you can purchase these boxes. You'll want to find one that blends with your décor since it will be sitting out.

Here's what you're going to need to whip your paper piles into shape:

- A desktop file box
- Set of hanging folders (any color)
- Pad of 2" x 2" sticky notes
- Pen
- Calendar

Here are the steps for dealing with any backlog of papers that may be sitting around:

1. Set your kitchen timer for eighteen minutes and jump in. No, you will not finish in eighteen minutes, but you'll make a serious dent.

2. Gather up a good-sized handful of pending paperwork from the countertops and tables. Do not pick them all up since you want to be able to start and finish in the small block of time. If you start with a huge pile, then you'll have to leave it undone, which leaves a bigger mess in your wake.

3. Sit down and separate it into piles of like papers, for example: all the bills, all the items to read, photos, coupons, receipts, and so on.

4. As you sort into piles, toss the no-brainer stuff like expired coupons. But do not get caught in decision making about the papers. This is not the time to decide to keep it or toss it. It is also not the time to think about if you do or do not want to go to the party you've been invited to. Instead, toss the invitation in the invitations pile and move on. It is also not the time to flip through catalogs or read magazines.

5. Once you have the large pile sorted into smaller piles with specific categories, you are almost done.

6. Next, grab a hanging folder and put all of one pile in the file.

7. Use a sticky note to label the file. Do this by sticking the sticky part of the note to the file and leave the rest sticking up as the label. There are no perfect label names, just write something that will help you remember what is inside. "Important," "pending," "this week," and "urgent" are not the best choices, since so many of the papers potentially fall in those categories. Instead, use names like, "sports schedules," "social invitations," "scouts," and so on. A more complete list of options is below.

8. The final step in the process is to note anything that needs your attention on the calendar. Since you are not going to want to have to sift through each file every day to see what needs your attention, you'll want to be prompted. So, let's say you need to sign your child up for swim lessons by the twentieth of the month. On the calendar write in a box

about a week earlier "swim sign up—paper in swim folder." When you look at your calendar that day you'll be reminded not only to sign up, but where the paper is. And since it will be about a week before the deadline, there will not be a last-minute rush.

9. During your next eighteen-minute block of time, go through another handful. Continue this process at least weekly until the backlog is gone and don't forget to maintain the box by dealing with incoming mail on a daily basis.

Here is an example of how a paper might flow through your new system.

The mail comes in today and you receive a community school brochure that you'd like to flip through. You may or may not register for a class; you need to read the brochure first. Open the brochure to the registration page to see what the date is to register by. Go to your calendar and write in a note about a week before the deadline to remind yourself to read the brochure and that it will be in the community school folder. Then, take a sticky note and write "community school" on it. Put the label in the file, put the brochure inside, and tuck it away. When the date rolls around you will see the note on the calendar reminding you that you need to read the brochure. At that point, carry the brochure with you so you can glance at it in your spare time. If nothing catches your eye then toss the brochure. If you see something you want to register for, either fill out the form and send the check in, or put it in the bill file to be paid in your next bill paying session. Write the date of the class on the calendar. Then, place the brochure back in the community school file, since you'll want to have it on hand to refer to the day of the class so you have all the pertinent information. Done!

These files live here a short time. The summer camp file stays only until you register for summer camp or camp is ended. But no longer. Other files, like bill and receipts stay but the contents only stay a little while. That is why you use the sticky notes instead of the plastic tabs. Since the file is temporary, there is no sense in wasting time making a file tab, although for the files that are long term categories, like "bills" and "receipts," you may choose to use the tabs, since the sticky notes will eventually fall off.

Here are some examples of what belongs in which basic folder:
- Household: warranties and instruction manuals
- To Read: magazine articles, newsletters
- Receipts: receipts
- Recipes: recipes
- Travel: brochures, other ideas
- Entertainment: tickets to events and newspaper clippings of upcoming ideas
- Bills: bills to be paid
- To File: select papers that will be moved to a permanent file
- Taxes: items needed for upcoming tax filing

- Contacts: business cards and scraps of paper with names and numbers
- Photos: to be put into an album
- Family Meeting: topics to be discussed
- Schedules: sports schedules, recycling calendars, event calendars
- Health: kids medical records, prescriptions, physician referrals
- Directions: either printed from the Internet or written down
- Social Engagements: party invitations, directions to the events
- Restaurants: restaurants you want to try and reviews
- Coupons: coupons and gift certificates
- Grocery Shopping: sales flyers, shopping list, food store coupons
- Discussion: things to ask your spouse about
- Day Trips: brochures and ideas of day trips to take
- Books to Read: lists of books you'd like to read one day and book reviews
- Movies to See: a list of movies you'd like to see and reviews of them
- Gifts: ideas of gifts to buy for others or a wish list for yourself, pictures clipped from catalogs stapled to the order information
- Instructions: clippings of a craft pattern, decorating a cake, or other directions
- Take-Out Menus: menus for the local restaurants and corresponding coupons
- Banking: deposit and withdrawal receipts, monthly statements to be reconciled
- Clippings: newspaper or magazine clippings

that do not fit another category but would be good to refer to at some point

- Online: websites that have been recommended to you or that you would like to check out one day
- Investments: brokerage house statements
- School: lunch tickets, school work in progress, school calendar
- Spiritual: schedules of events
- Memory Box: artwork and other items to be saved in a treasure box
- A file for each family member

Remember that your box will be personalized since every person has different categories of paper to deal with. You may have some or all of the ones above and others like "hairstyle ideas," "places to visit," "landscaping," "PTA," "Cub Scouts," "Bake Sale," "Kitchen Remodel," "Birthday Party," "Halloween Costumes," "Holiday Card Writing," "Getting Organized," and so on.

Lastly, this desktop file box works well for other areas of your life. You might opt to have one at work, or one for an organization you head, or one for your home business, and if you travel for work or run a scouting troop, one in the car as well might simplify your life. Maintaining the file box is easy; weed through it the same day(s) of the month you pay your bills, so you are sure to keep the files up to date and a manageable size.

And what should you do with all the papers that belong to your spouse or someone else in the house? Here is a no fail solution for those papers.

Take a three-tier organizer, and designate three categories, one per tier. An example would be, to read, to file, and to pay. Then make an agreement that when the "to read" tier is full you will toss out some items. This solution alleviates the need to continually ask that person "Do you need this?", "Can you move your papers off the table?", or "Are you done with this yet?" With a home for the papers, an agreement, and maintenance, this system will work.

One final paper wrangling solution is to group the papers together in a binder system. In a thin binder, a half inch to an inch, place a few sheet protectors, a few three-hole punched folders, and a three-hole punched pencil case. The folders are used instead of a three-hole punch because it is unrealistic to think that you will have the time to hole punch each paper to put in the binder. Then group all of one category in the binder—for example maybe the take-out menus. Then instead of fumbling through a bunch in a file you can slip each menu into a sheet protector and read the binder like you would a book. You could also create a binder for a remodeling project, with the plans and estimates in the folders, brochures in the sheet protectors, and paint chips and fabric swatches in the pencil case. For easy reference, be sure to label the spine of the binder. It's as easy as that!

28.
More Paper Tips

Resolve yourself to the fact that the papers need to be dealt with daily. The good news is you can keep on top of the paper pile in just eight minutes a day! Pick a time that is best for you to open and sort the mail. Eight minutes a day is far less than the hours it can take to go through an unwieldy pile at the end of the week or, gulp, month.

During your eight-minute block of time, open all the envelopes and sort the mail. A battery-operated letter opener is fun to use and makes the job go quicker. Because there is no exposed blade, the chore can be delegated to a child. During the eight minutes when you are ready to put the papers away, be sure you have everything you need. You'll want to have a garbage can handy, the shredder, your calendar, and the desktop file box. With your pile in hand, sort the papers. You only have three choices about what to do with each piece of paper. You can toss it out. (Take advantage of this option often.) You can file it away. Or you can keep it handy to take some sort of action, like pay the bill, RSVP to an invitation, register for a class, and so on.

Here are some other helpful ways to deal with the paper:

594. Stop what you can from coming in the first place. Request an email version of statements. Cancel catalog and magazine subscriptions. Whenever you give out your address, ask that your name not be used in a mailing list or sold to a third party.

595. Paper's golden rule: All paper belongs standing up vertically, not laying horizontally. Remember this and you will never make another pile of paper again.

BONUS TIP:
Place incoming mail into a napkin holder—this keeps the mail from becoming a pile.

596. There are three types of files that need to be kept. Confusing the types will lead to losing papers in the filing system. The first type is the active file, which is most likely going to be kept in the kitchen, or somewhere more centrally located than a home office. It includes all the current topics that are being worked on.

597.

The second type is the permanent file. This is the two or three drawer filing cabinet in a home office area where recently accessed files are kept. Examples are last year's tax return, the automobile insurance policy, health insurance information, and this year's bank statements.

BONUS TIP:

On the file tab write how long you need to keep the papers in the file. For example, the IRS recommends holding on to pay stubs for three years. So on the file tab, write the date after which you can get rid of the file. That way you'll always know what can be put through the shredder when it comes time to weed your files. See a full retention schedule on page 417.

598.

Archival filing is the third type. This is usually placed in an out of the way place such as the basement or attic. Many archival files are stored in banker's boxes instead of filing cabinets. Files that are commonly found here include the past six years of tax returns and the past six years of banking statements.

BONUS TIP:

Consider a shredding party. Finally get rid of those piles to be shred by inviting people to participate and charging a nominal fee that will cover the cost of hiring a mobile shredding company. Have the truck come and shred everyone's piles!

599. Disaster proof storage. Important and irreplaceable documents need to be stored in a way that they are protected from disaster. You may choose to keep these documents in a bank deposit box or at home in a safe or a disaster-proof box. If you choose to keep them yourself, be sure that the container is both fire and waterproof. Also, be sure it is large enough to house all the important documents. A list of recommended papers to place in disaster-proof storage is located in the reference section in the back of the book.

600. One way many charities and other companies make a significant amount of their money is to sell your name as part of a mailing list to other companies. This doesn't mean you should stop your charitable contributions; it just means you should ask them to refrain from selling your personal information.

601. If you opt to request that your statements be sent via email then consider setting up a second email address specifically for this purpose. Your personal or work email can quickly become overloaded with statements. To avoid that, register for a free email address and have statements sent there. Use this email address when placing orders; this way the confirmation information and tracking numbers do not clog your inbox.

602. Do not bring any mail into the house that you do not need. Take an extra moment outside and flip through it. Immediately toss all the stuff you know you do not want. It may help to have a recycling bin near the front door.

603. If you pick up your mail at a post box, do the same thing. Leave everything there that you do not want. Bring home only what you want to deal with.

604. Sensitive parts of documents, such as account numbers and other personal information should be safely destroyed. Keep a small box where you can toss items that need to be destroyed. Then make time to shred. If you keep on top of the to-be-shredded pile, it will never take very long.

605. If the piles of sensitive documents have gotten out of control and you need an industrial-strength shredder to catch up, consider hiring a shredding company. They come to your home and shred in the truck; they typically charge by the minute.

606. Shredding may be a task that you can delegate to someone else. Can an older child take it on as a chore? Can a babysitter shred for you as part of their routine?

607. To make shredding easy, keep a large, difficult-to-jam shredder in a convenient place. If it is easier to shred the papers as they come in the mail then place the shredder where you open mail; it may mean keeping it in the kitchen.

BONUS TIP:
Keep the shredder plugged in at all times, this makes it easier to shred and you will be more likely to do it. Keep it behind a childproof door if you have little children.

608. You may feel comfortable throwing away your sensitive papers if you just pour some bleach over them once they are in the bag. Another option is to compost them in your garden. Or, if you have a fireplace, you can use the paper as kindling.

609. Whenever you file, be sure to file for retrieval. There are no perfect file names. The name of the file has to make sense to you.

610. Use broad categories when filing. The more specific the name the less papers will fit in the category so you will end up with hundreds, if not thousands of files.

611. Use a single filing system. If you deviate from the system, it makes it virtually impossible to find the paper you need.

612. Make filing simple. The hanging folder will be the broad category, and inside will be all the file folders related to the broad subject. Take a hanging folder and give it a broad category such as "home." Then grab a file folder and write "warranties" on the tab and across the front. Then fill the file folder with all the warranties for household appliances. Next, add another file folder to the hanging folder and so on. Writing the category across the front of the file makes the name easy to read when you can't see the tab.

613. Don't feel you have to color code. It can sometimes be more trouble than it is worth. You might choose to use aqua colors for your household files. But then if you run out of aqua files you are either not going to file until you get more or you are going to use another color in the same category, blowing the whole system. Instead, just file. The one exception would be if you have two distinct categories, such as home stuff and a home-based business. That would be a good reason to use two colors. Keep plenty of empty files on hand and choose common colors so they are sure to still be in stock when you need more.

614. There is a better way to file all the files than just alphabetically. Store files first by category such as home, financial, children, auto, and so on. Then, within each category, file alphabetically. If you find yourself reaching for particular files often, then place those in the front. No sense having to pull open a drawer all the way to search for a file you need daily.

615. Sticky notes will become your new best friends. Once you review a paper and need to take an action, stick on a sticky note with the action required. That way, the next time you pick up the paper, you'll know exactly what to do, and you will not waste valuable time rereading.

616. Once you have read something and decide to file it, simply highlight the key word so you know where to file it. This will save you lots of time so you don't have to reread the paper to try to remember if you meant to save it, and if so, where you wanted to put it.

617. Create a file map of your filing cabinet. That way, in the event someone else needs to locate one of your papers in a emergency, they can do so. To create a file map, simply make a list of the files by file drawer; then, note where the disaster proof box and key are kept. Store the file map in the first file of the top drawer and tell everyone who needs to know where it is.

618. It's okay to cancel the subscriptions of the catalogs, magazines, and newspapers you are not reading. Instead, pick up the few you do want at the store and save your time and money.

619. You can pass along the subscription by calling the subscription department and changing the address to have it delivered to someone else. Some ideas are, a friend or a family member, your physician's office, a local hospital, a day care center, or an assisted living facility.

620. Create a new household rule—when a new catalog or magazine arrives, toss the old one. When the newspaper arrives, read it that day or toss it, whether or not it has been read.

621. Read what you can online—newspapers, magazines, recipes, etc.

622. To make keeping up with the reading material even easier, pull out articles and carry them with you. Slip them into a file labeled "to read" and bring it with you when there is a chance you'll have some spare time, like while sitting in a physician's waiting room waiting to be called.

623. When you pull a file out, mark the spot with a slip of paper; this makes refiling a snap.

624. Try living without a tray of papers to file. Instead, when you have a paper to file, do it right then. You will never have an unwieldy pile to file again. You'll never be searching through the pile for a paper that you need again. And it takes less time— try it.

625. When you put a new piece of paper into a file, place it in the front. So whenever you open a file the newest is in front.

626. Paper can be surprisingly heavy, be sure not to pack storage boxes of files so full that you are then unable to move them easily.

627. If you tend to need files or papers while you are traveling in your car then place a small file box in the car to keep them organized. For example, if you are a troop leader and need permission slips, directions, contact lists, and more, carry it all with you in a portable file box. Try to get a portable box with a lid so files don't dump out if the box tips over.

628. When you adjust the time on your clock to account for daylight savings, take a little while and weed your files.

629. Always leave space in the files to grow. You are going to get more paper, so leave a space for them. Otherwise, the file will be filled to the brim and you won't be able to file.

630. A good rule of thumb is that when a file reaches one inch in thickness, split it into two files.

631. If you are computer savvy, consider scanning some important documents onto your computer and tossing the paper copies.

632. Good questions to ask yourself are: "Can I get this somewhere else?" "Does someone else keep this?" "What's the worst that can happen if I toss this?" If you can get it somewhere else or you are okay living without it, then let it go.

633. Lateral filing cabinets are usually a better option compared to the vertical ones. A lateral drawer opens and you can see all the files. To get a file out of the back of a vertical filing cabinet, you need to extend the drawer fully. Plus, it can be hard to see the files in a four-drawer cabinet without a step stool.

634. When selecting a filing cabinet be sure that it offers the following options: drawers that extend fully, drawers that slide on ball bearings, a lock if you need one, and a track for hanging file folders.

635. Stacking trays in places by the printer, fax, and copier work well for papers needed often, like letterhead, envelopes, and fax covers.

636. A tickler file may work for you if you tend to need certain papers on specific days. Simply place thirty-one hanging folders in a desktop file box or in one drawer. Label the files one through thirty-one. Then, place papers in the file of the day you will need them. For example, if you have a wedding on the fifth of the month, place the invitation and directions in the five file. On the day of the wedding when you check your file for the day, the information you need will be there. The only way this system will work is if you check the file daily.

637. Once you check a receipt against your statement, you can toss it unless you need it for tax purposes or it was a big ticket item and you have a warranty. Toss cash receipts immediately, unless needed for tax purposes.

BONUS TIP:

Not sure what receipts you do and do not need? It is always recommended to ask your tax professional, and there is also a list in the appendix of this book. Ask your tax professional for a retention schedule so you are clear about what papers you do and do not need to hold onto.

638. If you are backlogged on files that need to be sorted through and weeded out, then go through one file a day until you get them all current. You're sure to find time to do one a day and you'll see progress within a few days—a much better solution than waiting for a block of time to get a bunch done.

639. Whenever you are working on a project create a new file folder and store all the related material in there. When you work on the project pull out the file and when you are done for the time being close the folder. This will keep all the pieces together. For example, if you are working on a billing dispute with your medical insurance company, create a new folder. You can keep all the notes, paperwork, and correspondences together. Once it is resolved, you can empty the file. Another example would be if you were planning a party. You could keep all your notes, guest lists, party ideas, contacts, and other associated paperwork together.

640. Use decorative file cabinets and bins. When you like the way it looks, it makes it more fun to use it.

641. If you have mail to pass along to another family member, perching it in a napkin holder can be a creative solution.

642. You can store the newest newspaper on the top of the recycling pile and get it only when you are ready to read it.

643. Do not read junk mail as you go through your mail, simply shred it.

644. You can remove yourself from the preapproved credit card solicitations lists by calling toll free 1-888-567-8688. This service is offered through the Federal Trade Commission and is highly rated by Consumer Reports.

645. You can also reduce the amount of junk mail you receive by up to 70 percent. All you need to do is send a signed letter to the Direct Marketing Association, Mail Preference Service, P.O. Box 643, Carmel, NY 15012, requesting your name be removed from the lists. You will have to make a note of all the ways the mail comes addressed to you. For example, Jane P. Smith, Jane Smith, J. Smith, and any misspelling such as Jone Smith and Janes Smith.

BONUS TIP:

If there is some junk mail you do like to receive, make a note of the items. That way if you are taken off those lists you can easily request to get back on those lists only.

BONUS TIP:

For the next month clip off the mailing information from the junk mail you receive. That way instead of rewriting all the ways junk mail comes addressed to you, you can simply staple the clippings to the letter.

646. Stop printing emails and Internet material. Instead, store it on the computer for future reference. For the emails, set up folders to cover the categories. Then move the email into the proper folder. Some examples are: joke of the day, "to do," to follow up on, soccer, from so-and-so, and recipes. And for the Internet material, you can store the file as a favorite link to go back to or keep the article itself. Create a folder in your word processing software and keep the article there.

647. There are two options for where to store papers you'll need in a few months. Examples are costume ideas for Halloween, a recipe for Mother's Day brunch, or a gift idea for the holidays. You can paper clip them to a wall calendar on the month that you will need them. Or you can give each category a file of its own such as, Halloween ideas, Mother's Day plans, or Holiday. Then store the folders in one area of a filing cabinet. To be sure they do not disappear into the black hole of the filing cabinet, write a note on the calendar to remind yourself that you have the file and where it can be located.

648. Forget about perfecting your system and having all the files labeled using a label maker. Most times this is a waste of time since files can change.

649. Staggering the file tabs across the files in the drawer causes you to spend time re-staggering them whenever you add a new file in the middle. Instead, opt to use the left hand for files labeled A–H, the center section for files labeled I–P, and the right hand side for files labeled Q–Z.

650. Avoid using paper clips when you are filing, it is easy for other unrelated papers to attach themselves. Instead, staple papers together.

651. Prepare a few extra empty folders that can be used to file in the future when you are in a rush. This avoids creating a pile of papers to be filed.

652. Use a red pen to list a destroy date on files. This makes purging your file drawers a snap. Instead of having to look at every paper in every file, you can simply scan the drawer and pull out the ones whose dates have passed. For example, the file of banking statements from 2001 can have a destroy date of January 2008. No need to can the file; simply shred the entire bunch.

653. You will find yourself making new files often and to make it super easy you'll want to have all the supplies needed on hand. Keep your marker, sticky notes, file tabs, and so on nearby.

654. You have two size options for size tabs on the file folders. One third cut and one fifth cut. This refers to the number of tabs that will fit across a single file, either three or five. The one third cut gives you a larger tab to write on so you can name the file more specifically plus you can write larger for more legibility.

655. File folder manufacturers have recently added a user-friendly file tab version to their file line. Look for smart tabs, these hanging files already have the plastic tabs attached across the width of the file, you simply pop up the one that is located in the position you desire.

656. Filing supplies is one area in which you don't want to skimp. Saving a dollar on a box of files can cost you much more in the long run. Less expensive files often cannot hold as much, forcing you to use more files; plus, the metal can bend and the paper can rip. Replacing broken files is more time consuming than doing it right the first time.

657.

Box bottom files are hanging folders that have a creased bottom allowing you to store many more file folders inside them. Box bottoms are not a great choice for regular filing because unless they are full, files tip back making the labels difficult to read. Reserve box bottoms for only the files where you have many folders. Or choose to make two hanging folders for the same topic, and forgo the box bottom option altogether.

TOSS

No brainer toss list: Expired files, business cards for people you do not remember, outdated letterhead with incorrect contact information, investment company prospectus, and supplies for office machines you no longer own.

29.

In the Home Office

658. You're running a household, so the first thing you need is a desk. Sorry, but you can no longer use the dining room table to stack papers and then push them aside when it's time to set the table for dinner. Be creative when choosing a desk. It doesn't have to be a traditional desk. You can buy an ornate one, or if space is tight, consider a desk that folds up or can be rolled out of the room. Your "command center" needs to be stocked with the following items: paper, sticky notes, ruler, scissors, crayons, glue or glue stick, pencils, colored pencils, pencil sharper, stapler, staple remover, tape, calculator, Wite-Out, and any other items you use daily.

659. An office area in some form needs to be near where the action happens in your home, usually the kitchen. You may have a home office on the second floor or in the basement, but there is no way you can run there all the time. To make life easy you need a mini office near the kitchen. And if you don't have a room to designate as the home office then one of these mini-office solutions will work well for you.

660. Use a closet. Take out the contents of the closet and take off the door. Slide in a desk or install a shelf as the desktop. You can add shelving that will give you more storage options. You can slide in a rolling cart under the shelf and roll it out when in use. Don't forget to add a light. To finish it off, hang a tension shower curtain rod and slip on a tabbed curtain so the office can be disguised when not in use.

661. Another option if you lack a convenient home office is to use a computer armoire. These pieces have doors that open and offer lots of storage inside. Even if you do not plan to put a computer inside it still functions as a workspace.

662. If you have no space for an armoire and cannot afford to lose a closet, then consider a simple rolling desk. You can wheel the desk out of sight when not in use, but as needed you can roll it up to the kitchen or dining room table as your workspace.

663. Another option for a small kitchen area is to use a cabinet. Place cork tiles on the back wall behind the shelf for a bulletin board.

664. As a last resort, the inside of a cabinet door will work as a makeshift office. Simply paint an area with chalkboard paint, or hang a few cork tiles or a whiteboard. Then hang a few tiered file holders that you can use to store different categories of papers.

665. Keep your desktop clear of clutter. Pens and notepaper can go in the top drawer along with the stapler and other essentials. Use the space as a workspace instead of a storage area.

666. To maximize your desk space and minimize distractions, keep the inbox off your desk. The inbox is meant for incoming items, and they come in by the door. So place your inbox closer to the door; that way as you walk by you can toss something in the box.

667. If the inbox consistently becomes a dumping ground of unfinished and "to do" projects then consider not having an inbox at all. Instead, deal with incoming papers as they arrive and put them in their home immediately.

668. Get to know your prime real estate. Keep items you use daily within arms reach. Then work outward from there. The items you use weekly should be stored where you can get them without getting up from your chair. The items you use less often can be stored where you'd have to get up to get them.

669. Designate one area as the supply zone. One bin, shelf, or large basket will work. This is where you should store all the extra office supplies. When you need something you can shop at home first, and when you are placing an order or writing a shopping list, you can easily check what you need to replace.

670. Make reordering a breeze by writing a simple list of the items and storing it by the supplies. Then, when you need to place an order, you can simply check off what you are running low on.

671. Using a hands-free headset allows you to multitask while on the phone. It is also keeps you from straining your neck.

672. Rolling file trolleys are a good solution if you need a bunch of files for a project. The files will be close at hand when needed, but not all over your desk.

673. To manage all the business cards you receive, you can either staple them into a Rolodex or slip them into a business card holder.

674. Get in the habit of writing the date on the back of business cards when they are given to you. Then, when you look at it later on, you'll know when you picked it up and how outdated it is.

675. Remember that leaving things to the last minute can be costly. Shipping packages overnight and buying supplies and having them rush shipped are two examples. Check your supplies weekly and reorder before it becomes an emergency and you spend money on a rush shipment on a printer ink cartridge. To avoid last minute shipments, try using online shipping. Simply log onto www.usps.gov or one of the other major shipping companies. Follow the directions to select your preferences and pay for shipment. A shipping label will print, and a company representative will come to pick up the package. In many cases you can leave the package for pick up if you will not be home at the designated time.

676. A lateral filing cabinet can double as an additional work surface. Just use caution so it does not become a catchall.

677. Clip groups of paper together using a binder clip. Label the clip with the action you need to take—file, pay, sign, do, and so on.

678. Create a reference library for all the instruction manuals you want to keep. If they are oddly shaped, store them in magazine holders by category—games, software, and so on. Placing them by category in sheet protectors in a three ring binder is another option.

BONUS TIP:
Keep in mind that many of the instruction manuals are available on the company's website, so you might choose to toss some knowing all the information is available online.

679. Professional journals can quickly go from enjoyable to overwhelming. To avoid unread stacks of them sitting around, try asking your local library to put them in circulation. That way you can read them if you choose to and in the meantime others can be enjoying them as well. On the other hand, you can choose to scan the table of contents and pull out any articles of interest. Lastly, you can opt to purchase two magazine holders, then place one years worth per holder, label the holders, and keep only that many for reference. Remember that 97 percent of what is filed is never referenced again, so truthfully, if you needed that information in the future, wouldn't you just research to find the most up-to-date information at that time?

680. Give everyone in the house a tray for papers, including kids, as soon as they are old enough to take on the responsibly of checking their own trays.

681. Silverware trays, typically used in the kitchen, work well in office desk drawers as dividers and organizers.

682. To make more room on your desk, remove photo frames. Instead, tuck the photos behind the ribbon on a French bulletin board.

683. Shy away from using bulletin boards, magnetic boards, or whiteboards, unless they are for a specific purpose. Hanging one up without a specific purpose leads to them becoming a cluttered storage area for outdated items when they are not kept current.

684. A task board is an all right choice, as long as it has a purpose and is maintained often to keep it up to date.

685. Keep the reference sheets and phone lists you use most often at your fingertips by storing them by the phone. Place them in a sheet protector and hang them up by the phone and keep one in your car so you'll never have to search for a phone number.

BONUS TIP:
Jot down the hours of operation so you never go to a store only to find that they are closed.

686. Have an oversized garbage can, without a lid nearby, and use it often.

687. Keep two smaller garbage cans next to the trash can to collect items to be shredded and recycled.

688. To take papers and files with you when you leave the house use a clear envelope with a tie closure or a clear zippered pouch. You can then grab it and go. The key is to empty the envelope or pouch when you are done so you can use it again.

689. Keep a can of keyboard cleaner handy. The nozzle allows you to spray pressurized air around the keys to blow out all the dust and crumbs.

690. As a safety measure, store backup copies of software and irreplaceable files on backup CDs in a disaster-proof box.

691. Screw a magnetized piece of metal sheeting to the wall near your desk. Then store miscellaneous items in metal tins with magnets on the back. Paper clips, push pins, and stamps all work well in the tins.

692. Keep important documents that you refer to often or personal items such as photographs up and off the desk by stringing a clothesline near your desk and clipping the items you need to the line.

693. Minimize horizontal surfaces, they tend to just be catchalls for clutter.

694. The floor is not an option. Period.

695. Make it a habit to clear your caller ID box. This can even be one of the chores delegated to a family member.

696. Since people's contact information can change, write their names in your address book in pen. But fill in their address, phone number, and email address in pencil. That way if information changes you can erase it instead of crossing it out.

BONUS TIP:

Collect all the scraps of paper you have hanging around with updates you want to make to your address book, then carry the book with you and make a few updates every time you have a spare moment. Maybe while waiting in a physician's waiting room, waiting to pick up a child from practice, or while watching television. The stationery and office supply company Levenger sells an address book with replaceable cards.

697. Another option for an address book is to store it on the computer. It would allow you to use the search function to find someone within the database, and make changes easily.

BONUS TIP:

Even if you do not store all your contacts on the computer, create a list with friends and family so you can print out labels for holiday cards.

698. Keep track of things you want to do, like trips you'd like to take, movies you'd like to see, books you'd like to read, restaurants you'd like to eat at, and so on. You can make a list and clip it to your calendar or have one file per category.

699. Write a list of the friends your child likes to schedule play dates with. Then post the list near the phone so it is handy.

700. When you print a copy of directions stop holding onto directions printed off the Internet. Instead store them on the computer and print as needed.

701. When sending someone directions to your home, include a picture of your house so they can spot it easily.

702. Register your phone numbers, including your cell phone number, on the do not call registry at www.donotcall.gov to stop telemarketers from soliciting you.

703. All-in-one or multifunction office machines save space.

704. Control all the wires and cords by wrapping them in a cord bundler. In addition, clip on a cord labeler so you know what cord belongs to what item.

705. Keep track of the websites you want to visit in a folder labeled "websites to visit." Whenever you have a spare moment to surf online you can pull out the file.

706. Once you have visited a website and you want to remember it, store the site in your favorites. Create a new folder for the category and then place the site in the folder.

707. Store books in your office by category. You can use a bookshelf and keep like with like, all the reference books together, and so on. If you are short on storage space for books remember to think vertical, use the floor to ceiling space. Another option is to install shelves around the perimeter of the office about eighteen inches from the ceiling.

708. Have office supplies delivered by ordering online. No more lugging home heavy cases of paper, and for orders over a certain dollar amount shipping is usually free.

709. Stop running to the post office to pick up stamps. Have them delivered from the U.S. Postal Service by calling 1-800-782-6724. Often, you can pick them up at the grocery store checkout or have them dispensed at your ATM machine.

710. If you like to save the boxes from expensive purchases that may need to be returned, you can do so without taking up a lot of space. Discard the packing material and fold down the box, then put a date on it when you'd feel comfortable throwing it away if you have not needed to return the item. Keep all these boxes on one shelf so you'll always know where they are in the event you need one.

711. To avoid spending hours on the computer or working in the office, set a timer. Hours can slip away without you realizing it. The buzz of the timer will keep you on track and make you more aware of how much time has passed.

712. Schedule time to deal with office tasks like filing, making and returning calls, responding to emails, and so on. Doing these tasks consistently will avoid the pile up when it takes hours to get through the backlog.

TOSS

No-brainer toss list: Office supplies that are unusable, outdated software, pens that no longer work, and dried out highlighters.

30.
Computers

713. Install a spam blocker to stop unwanted emails. Not having to delete them will save you time and keep your inbox freed up. Plus, you greatly lessen your chances of opening a virus-infected email.

714. Register for a free email account that you will give out when shopping online or creating a user ID on websites. This one you can check less often and it keeps your personal email account free of the clutter.

715. Make it a new rule to only check your email two times a day. Anything more is distracting and a waste of your time.

716. If your challenge is not checking it often enough, make it a new rule to check your email on the even days of the month.

717. To help clear your inbox, set your email options to have certain email delivered directly to a specific folder. For example, you can name a folder for an association you belong to, and then any emails from the members will be directly placed in that folder.

718. Stop signing up for all sorts of daily and weekly e-zines, jokes of the day, and horoscopes. Be selective and choose only the ones you really wish to receive.

719. Adjust your email setting to include an automatic signature on each of your emails. You can include your name and any other information you commonly give out. You can also add a line requesting that the recipient not add your name to broadcast emails such as jokes of the day.

720. Is your email inbox clogged up with a bunch of broadcast email? If so, compose a simple email asking that the sender remove you from their list.

721. You can write "no reply needed" at the end of emails when you do not need the recipient to reply. This avoids you getting back an email that simply says "thank you" or has a smiley face.

722. Files in the family computer can get just as disorganized and hard to find as anything else in the house. Give each family member his or her own folder on the desktop. Each person can then save files inside their designated folder.

723. As often as possible, choose the same user name and password. Then jot down the information in a Rolodex or address book designated for the Internet. Take QVC for example. You can put QVC.com under the Qs and note your user name and password. You may also want to jot down their 1-800 number in case you need to contact them. The next time you log on to browse or do some shopping, you'll have all the necessary information readily available. You won't waste time looking for scraps of paper or trying out variations of your name to guess what you chose.

724. Once you read an email avoid leaving it in your inbox. Instead, move the email to a file folder within your email program. You can create a new folder in a matter of seconds. Create a few with broad categories such as "follow up," "waiting to hear back," "associations," and so on. Weed these folders monthly; in the meantime, enjoy your clear inbox!

725. Online backup storage offers you a way to store your files securely without having to purchase external backup hardware.

726. Depending on how much space you have, it might make sense to store software CDs and the related papers in their original box on a shelf. If space is an issue, then toss the original box, unless you may need to return the product; in that case take the packing out of the box and break it down. Then store the CD in the jewel case.

727. Any spare computer equipment you have can be placed in a bin of its own and stored out of the way. If you need another mouse, keyboard, or cable you know where to look first.

728.
Stop printing emails. Read what you can online. Printing them only wastes your ink and does not mean that it is read any sooner. Besides, you can opt to save them on your computer by copying them into a file or bookmarking the link.

TOSS
No-brainer toss list: Files on the computer that are outdated, older versions of software, software you never use, and books you do not want any longer.

31.

At the Office

729. Do not leave chairs near your desk; they just become clutter hot spots because they are so tempting to drop things onto.

730. Keep items you use daily within reach and items you use weekly close by. Stuff you use less often can be stored someplace you have to get up to get to.

731. Don't have your desk facing the door. Facing the door and looking up as people pass is distracting. Plus, it encourages unwelcome visitors to stop in and chat.

732. If you remember something you need to do while you're working, jot it down instead of switching tasks. It may seem harmless enough to stop your work just to type a quick email, but that's never the case. You open your email to compose a letter and then see that you have messages. Next thing you know you are reading incoming emails and dealing with new issues and have abandoned your original project.

733. At the end of each day spend time preparing for the next day, gathering everything you'll need and putting away everything you won't.

734. Give each project a deadline, even if it's self-imposed.

735. To keep papers related to separate projects from mixing, give each project its own folder. Place the name of the project on the folder and use the same name for the project files on the computer.

736. Put away projects even when they are in mid-process and you intend to go back to them. For instance, don't leave a report sprawled across your desk when you go to attend a scheduled meeting. Though you may have every intension of getting right back to it, this will probably not happen. So, place the report in the project file and put the file away before the meeting.

737. Using a timer during tasks goes a long way to helping you stay on track. You're much more aware of time if a clock is ticking down. Tasks will usually expand to fill the amount of time you've allotted for them. If you have a five-page report to write and you have all day, it will probably take you that long. And if you have just the morning it will probably take you that amount of time.

TOSS
No-brainer toss list: Dried up pens with no ink, outdated files, and pads of paper with five or less sheets of paper on them.

32.

Tips for the Home-Based Business

738. Since you are running a business, you will need a workspace separate from the living space in your home. Designate a space that can be used for business only.

739. If your business requires you to carry inventory be sure to store like items together and label everything for easy reference.

740. Use a second no fail desktop file solution for your business.

741. Place business appointments on the family calendar to avoid double booking. Use a different colored pen, or highlight the business appointments.

742. When you make a business appointment, jot the phone number next to the appointment so you can easily call to confirm or make a change.

TOSS

No-brainer toss list: Old versions of your business card, outdated files, duplicate office supplies, printer supplies for a printer you no longer own, and old versions of software.

Part Nine:

Storage Areas

Storage areas are so often ignored since we visit them so infrequently. Still they deserve to be treated as part of the house. All too often stuff is just thrown in and the door is quickly pulled shut. It doesn't have to be that way.

It is actually a very efficient use of your time to take a few moments and store something so you can find it again instead of the alternative, which is to toss and go. If you don't store properly, when you need the item it takes a search party to rescue it from the depths of the piles. Sometimes you may forget you own it or abandon the search and go buy another one.

To avoid leaving good items stranded in storage, here are some simple solutions that will keep your storage areas as organized as the living space in your home.

33.
Attics and Basements

743. To make retrieving bins very easy, you can install a bin rack. The rack can be anchored to the wall to avoid it tipping forward. The rack allows you to store one bin per cubby instead of simply piling bins on top of each other. Piling them makes it difficult to get to the ones below and can crush the contents.

744. An alternative to the bin rack is simple plastic or metal shelving units. The shelving units on locking casters are the best option since you'll be able to move them around even when they are full.

745. Sensitive materials, like photos, musical instruments, collectables, books, multimedia, and other treasures should not be stored in areas where there can be drastic temperature changes, humidity, and pest problems. Be careful what you store where, and always be sure it is stored in proper containers.

746. Compact dehumidifiers are available, including hanging versions. Bundling sticks of chalk together with a rubber band and hanging them is a low cost version.

747. Group all containers of the same kind together—all holiday decorations, all out of season clothing, all baby items, and so on. Stack all like items together, or finding things will be time-consuming and frustrating.

748. Inside the storage containers, continue storing like with like. For example: all the holiday tree decorations or all the newborn baby items. That way, when you need to pull something out, you don't have to dig through to find what you need. When you need the items to trim the tree, they will all be together instead of commingled with all the other holiday decorations. And when you need newborn items, they will all be together instead of mixed in among items for all age groups.

749. Store all the items that belong together away together. For example, if you have a specialty soap dispenser for Halloween then pack it away with the Halloween decorations. Otherwise, it will be in your way all the other months of the year.

750. Store holiday-themed photo frames in with the holiday items. You can even store the frames with photos inside. Then when you pull out the decorations you'll already have photos of holiday memories gone by.

751. When you store clothing, separate them by size, gender, and season. Making many smaller bins allows you easy access to the items you want. You won't have to dig through large bins to find what you need. Label each bin with the size and the type of contents.

752. Use the same method when storing toys. Make many smaller bins instead of a few larger ones. Separate the toys by age and type. For example, place all newborn toys in one bin and in another bin place toddler toys. Label each bin clearly before storing it away.

753. Don't hold onto things that have a tendency to change safety standards, like car seats, cribs, and ride on toys. Also, remember items can be recalled, so you'll need to commit to staying current with the recall notices.

754. Before storing posters in cardboard tubes and framed artwork in bubble wrap, take a photo of each. Then tape the photo to the wrapped piece and write a small description. Then you will not have to unwrap it to figure out what is inside.

755. Make a summer fun section in the storage area. This is where you can place all the items you'll want to use during the summer months: plastic daiquiri glasses, palm tree serving platters, and more. By putting them away, you will not clutter your cabinets during the times of the year when you don't use them.

756. Paint colors on walls fade after only six months because of sunlight and other elements. So, if you were to do a touch up, the paint color will not match. Don't hold onto half full paint cans for touch ups, since you'd need to repaint the entire room anyway. Instead, save only a baby jar full for mini touch ups. Label the jar with the room where you used the paint.

757.
If you still want to hold onto the paint cans, label each can with the name of the room in which you used it. Also draw a line on the outside to mark the level of paint inside, and then you won't have to open it to see how much is left.

TOSS

No-brainer toss list: Cans of paint colors you no longer use, cracked containers or bins, clothing that is being stored but will not be used, and items stored for which safety standards have changed.

34.

Closets of
All Kinds

758. Custom closets are a popular way to go. They allow you to maximize the closet space by going floor to ceiling and adding tons of shelf space. The best part is that the unit is designed specifically for your needs.

759. If a custom closet is out of your budget you can create your own version of a custom closet with store-bought pieces. The single rod and shelf above it will need to come out of the closet. Replace it with a combination of tall, thin shelving, rolling carts, double hanging rods, and shoe shelves.

760. If you have metal shelving and your things slip through the gaps, you can make it more functional by adding shelving liners.

761. Design your closet how the stores do. Place like with like. For example, keep all the skirts next to each other and all your casual pants separate from your dress pants. You can even go so far as to line each item up by color under each category. That way it is a cinch to find a short-sleeve white T-shirt and a pair of jeans.

762. The wire hangers the dry cleaners use can end up in knots, but there is a product on the market designed specifically to hold hangers. You can place the hangers on the organizer to reuse them, or place them on the organizer so it is easy to tie them up neatly for recycling.

INSIDER TIP:
Some dry cleaners will reuse them or recycle them for you. Some dry cleaners will also place your clothing on your hangers if you bring them in.

763. Navy and black pieces can be difficult to tell apart especially inside a dark closet. To make the differentiation easier, use a different color hanger for navy items.

764. Keep a bag in the bottom of the closet where you can toss items that you're going to be donating. Once the bag is full, you can call to have a charity near you pick it up. Or you might prefer to place it in the trunk of your car. Then you can drop it off the next time you're near a donation site.

765. To find out what clothing you actually wear, hang all the hangers on the rod backwards. Then, as you wear the item, place the hanger on the rod the right way. In a few weeks, you will have a true sense of what you are really wearing.

766. Take all but five of the hangers you are not using out of the closet and store them somewhere else. You will instantly gain more closet space. Before you do, remember to calculate how many you will need to hang up the clothing that is currently in the laundry.

767. If you find it difficult to see into the depths of your closet because it is too dark, add a light. There are battery-operated lights that can hang on the wall or ceiling. You can also opt for adding a regular light bulb with a plunger so it automatically goes on whenever you open the closet door and turns off when the door is shut. If you are going to add a light bulb consult a licensed electrician so you can follow the fire codes and regulations.

768. Keep in mind that the space right in front of you at arms reach when you open your closet is the prime space. Place items you use daily there. Work outward from there, placing the rarely used items highest and lowest in the closet.

769. If you are storing items in the back of the closet or up high on shelves, avoid forgetting what is tucked away by jotting it on a piece of paper and taping the paper to the inside of the closet door.

770. Day of the week cubbies work well in children's closets. The five or seven space cubby organizer simply attaches over the rod with Velcro. Each cubby can be filled with the day's outfit and other items needed that day.

771. Men's ties work best on a spinning tie rack. If there are ties that are really meant to be worn only at certain times of the year, then store them away with the out of season clothing or with the holiday decorations, leaving the tie rack full of ties that can be worn now.

772. Belts can be stored on a belt organizer, on hooks screwed into the inside of the door, or slipped onto "S" hooks tightened around the rod in the closet.

773. If the top shelves of your closet are difficult to reach then store a slim step stool in the closet. That way you can use the entire closet and eliminate unusable space.

774. Fold up a few tote bags and store them in a large tote bag. You only need five so choose ones in a variety of sizes, shapes, colors, and materials.

775. You can instantly double the hanging space in your closet by simply hanging a double hang bar from the rod in your closet.

776. Store central vacuum hoses and accessories in a closet near the hookup. Wrap the hose around a garden hose organizer and place attachments in a plastic shoe holder hung on the back of the door.

777. Make your closet current. Fill it with all the items you use and love today. Tuck memory items in a memory bin. Store away clothing that may fit you again one day and take out the out of season clothing. You can even take out the fancy gowns and other rarely used items and hang them in another closet. This will get you back your valuable closet space and make it simple to put away the laundry.

778. Store the sheet sets for the bed in your closet. Having them handy makes changing the bed a lot easier. Place the flat sheet and the bottom sheet along with the pillow-cases inside one of the pillow cases, that way all the matching pieces are kept together. Plus they stack more easily that way.

BONUS TIP:
Keep only the sheet sets that you like and that fit well. And keep only a few sets—how many do you really use?

779. Collect all the articles of clothing that are memorabilia and not things you wear. These do not belong in your closet and dresser drawers taking up valuable space. They belong in a memory bin.

780. While weeding through the clothing, a great question to ask yourself so you know what to purge is, "Would I buy this again today?" If the answer is no, then part with it immediately.

BONUS TIP:

Two other questions to ask yourself are, "Do I feel good when I wear this?" and "Is it easy to wear and care for?"

781. Use drawers and baskets on tracks that glide out for easy use.

782. Place a small pop-up hamper, or a canvas-lined basket in the closet to collect dirty clothes.

783. Use the valuable space on the inside of the closet door. You can hang an over the door organizer or hooks that will hold a variety of items including hats, purses, belts, and scarves. The same organizers come in over-the-rod versions.

784. Bi-fold or pocket doors are the best choice for closet doors because they will maximize the amount of useable space. Sliding doors do not allow you to see the center of the closet without having to slide the doors back and forth.

785. If you prefer to store your shoes in their boxes then tape a photo of each pair to the box. Or use a clear plastic box you can see through.

786. Use a baseball cap rack to hang the hats. One version has clips and hangs on the inside of the door, another version hangs from the rod, and a third option nests the hats inside one another and hangs them in a stack.

787. Store wide-brimmed hats in hat-boxes. Stack them on the top shelf of the closet. Label each one clearly and tape a photo of the hat to the outside of the box.

788. If an outfit comes with accessories keep them with the outfit by placing them in a small bag and hanging the bag on the hanger with the rest of the ensemble.

789. Brooches and pins stick well to a heavyweight ribbon hanging on the inside of the closet door.

790. Hanging a full-length mirror on the inside or over the closet door keeps it out of sight until you are getting dressed.

791. Unless you have overnight guests visiting weekly, do not set aside an entire closet for them. It will waste valuable space. Instead, use the closet and when guests are due to arrive carve out a small section for them to use.

792. Before you hang up clothing, empty out the pockets.

793. Do not put anything away if it is in need of repair, is stained, or does not fit well.

794. Wire hangers are not sturdy, they often chip paint off the rod and can leave pull marks in the clothing. Choose to use a higher quality plastic hanger or a non-slip version.

795. An inexpensive improvement that makes your closet much more functional is a rod cover which helps hangers glide along the rod easily.

796. Make a new household rule about the dry cleaning. In our home, we do not hang the dry cleaning in the closet until the bags are taken off. Not only do the bags clutter the closet but they are also bad for the clothing; the chemicals stay trapped in the bag and can damage the fabric.

797. An easy way to hang all your accessories is to place a pegboard on one wall of the closet. On the hooks you can hang purses, belts, scarves, hats, and much more.

798. Write what item the replacement button or spare length of thread belongs to as soon as you snip it off. Then store all these packets in one envelope in your dresser drawer or a small tin. If you ever need a button you can find it instead of looking through all of them wondering what they belong to.

799. Not sure what to do with the clothing that is a size or two too big or too small for you or your child? A very easy solution is to store it away. Get it out of the drawers and off the closet shelves. It is taking up valuable real estate. Group sizes together in containers. Label each container and tuck it away. Then, if and when you need that size, you can pull out the containers. Only place clothes in the container that are stain free, need no repair, and are easy to care for. No sense holding onto a hand wash only dress that you only sort of like and that needs a button replaced.

800. Once your child has outgrown an item or no longer uses something, take it out of the closet. If an item holds a special memory then place it in the memory bin. For example, his or her first pair of shoes can be placed in a memory bin, but they should not be kept in the closet. It makes it more difficult to find the shoes that do fit and you run the risk of the memory piece being ruined.

801. Separate your gift wrap and gift bags into two or three categories: holiday, birthday, and other. Store the holiday gift wrap with the holiday decorations. Keep the other types handy. A shallow, under-the-bed, rollaway gift wrap organizer is one solution. Another is the standing version. Both of these styles offer an area to stow scissors, bows, and ribbon.

Coupon cutters slice the paper cleanly and, unlike scissors, have no exposed blades.

802. Gift bags can be tucked under the rolls of gift wrap if you are using the flat organizer. Bags do not work well in the standing up version; they are often crushed to the bottom when you put a roll of paper back on top of them. You can place all the gifts bags inside the largest of the gift bags. You can also stand them up in a box or buy a gift bag organizer. This is a pop-up bag with slots for various size bags. Be sure to separate your bags by category; it will make it much easier to find them.

803. During the holidays when you'll be wrapping many gifts, designate one area as gift wrap central. Place all the supplies there so you have everything you need when you go to wrap a gift, including to/from tags.

804. Designate one shelf of a closet to be the gift shelf. This is where you can store all the gifts you buy to give at a future date or items you have set aside as last minute generic gifts such as gift cards and art sets.

805. On the same shelf, you can also store a box with greeting cards in it. Use dividers to separate the categories. Then the next time you need a card you do not have to run out to the store.

806. After you wear an article of clothing, it might not be dirty enough to be laundered but you may not want to put it back in the closet to mingle with the clean clothes. You can designate one area of the closet for worn items so they are tucked away but not mixed in with clean items.

807. Do not clutter up your linen closet with seasonal items, like beach towels. Instead, store the seasonal items all by themselves.

808. Keep your front closet clear by having a plan. Use all the space by going to the ceiling with the shelving where you can store out of season items. Limit the number of coats, shoes, and accessories each person can store there. Keep only the commonly-used items in the front hall closet and tuck other items in storage.

TOSS

No-brainer toss list: Clothing you no longer love, out of style belts, sheets with holes in them, gift wrap too wrinkled to use, and shoes that have seen better days.

35.

Garage

809. The first step is to plan what activities you and other family members engage in that require equipment. Then, depending on what time of year you need what equipment, you can plan how to use the space you have in the garage.

810. Label all the storage areas including the shelves.

811. Hang what you can, including ladders.

812. Roll extension cords up and loop them over a nail on the wall.

813. Hang a slat wall or grids on one or more walls. You can then slip in baskets and other organizers that are designed to hold a variety of items, including gardening supplies, sporting equipment, and much more.

814. Separate small items like nails and bolts; you can use a caddy with small pullout drawers or place them in jars that you can label with masking tape.

815. Consider adding durable flooring to all or some areas of the garage floor.

816. Just because it is a garage doesn't mean it shouldn't be decorative. Paint it a fun vibrant color.

817. Add a high quality mat in front of the door so no dirt is tracked inside.

818. Better yet, leave shoes in the garage by creating a small mudroom area. If you do not already have an official mudroom, consider placing an armoire in the garage to collect backpacks, umbrellas, coats, and shoes before they make their way inside.

819. If your valuable garage space is being taken up with other people's belongings then give everyone a deadline to pick up stuff or give it away without feeling guilty since they had a fair chance. Besides, how much could it really mean to them if they just dumped it anyway?

820. Before you store sporting equipment, look through what you own. Keep only what you truly use and what is in good working order. Then store like with like. Label everything so you know what you have and can retrieve it easily.

821. Once seasonal equipment is separated by category and contained in bins it can be stored. Be sure the bins are clearly labeled on all sides.

822. Use the overhead space. Install a rack that hangs from the rafters.

BONUS TIP:
Measure first to be sure your car will still fit underneath.

823. Create a recycling center. Designate one bin for each category. Leave string and scissors handy to bundle newspapers if required. Post the recycling schedule on the wall after you have made a note of it on the family calendar.

824. Hang helmets on the handlebars of each bicycle.

825. Leave items you want children to be able to reach themselves at their level.

826. Tape the needle for an air pump to the pump itself so you'll always have it when you need it.

827. Balls, bats, Frisbees, and other such sporting equipment store well in milk crates or pop-up totes.

828. Hula-hoops are best hung from a hook on the wall.

829. Pop-up huts and play tents can be difficult to fit back into the case they were originally packaged in. Consider folding them up and slipping them into an extra large Ziploc bag—one of the newer products on the market.

830. Kiddie pools can be left blown up. Use a bungee cord to tie them up on a wall of the garage after they are dry.

831. Store all dangerous items such as radiator fluid and sharp tools out of a child's reach. You can even use a locking cabinet to make the items doubly secure.

832. Whenever you take down storm doors or screens label them immediately with their appropriate location. It will make it so much easier to put them back up when the time comes.

833. Separate children's toys by category—water, sporting, and so on. Then store like with like.

834. A simple way to get ride on toys out from underfoot is to use painter's tape to make "parking spaces" on the garage floor.

TOSS
No-brainer toss list: Rusted tools and garden equipment, broken toys, sidewalk chalk less than an inch long, deflated balls that cannot be reinflated, fluid and oils that are expired or have too little left to save.

36.

Patio, Shed, and Pool

835. Pool supplies should be separated by category—chemicals, accessories, etc.—then placed up and out of the way so children cannot reach them. Also, keep the instructions for pool equipment and cleaning directions in with the pool supplies so you do not have to search for them.

836. Pool toys that are easy to deflate and reinflate should have the air taken out of them.

837. Use pop-up totes to store the pool toys.

838. Patio furniture can be brought into the shed or garage during the off months. Some chairs can nest onto one another, and other furniture can be hung from the walls and ceiling. Be sure everything is clean and dry before storage to avoid mildew growth.

839. BBQ utensils and accessories are best kept out of kitchen drawers. Use the drawers for items you need daily, and place these specialty items in a tote bag that can be hung near the BBQ area or in a plastic tub with a locking lid. Label the container and store it on a shelf in the garage.

840. If you opt for a shed, then use it for only one or two groups of items rather than as another miscellaneous dumping area. A shed can be for lawn maintenance equipment, gardening supplies, children's toys, or a workshop. Trying to make a small shed function in many ways spells disaster.

TOSS
No-brainer toss list: Duplicate toys, blow up toys with holes in them, rusted BBQ utensils, BBQ covers with holes in them.

Part Ten:

Financial Clutter

These techniques will instantly whip your financial papers into order. You can't be financially sound or have a plan to get out of debt until you clear up financial clutter. Having simple systems to deal with incoming bills, bank accounts, and investments is a must. The great news is that you do not have to have a degree in finance to be able to clear up the clutter. Even if you've never balanced a checkbook, these solutions work.

Imagine the freedom from wondering if the bills have been paid—no more late fees, and the end to stressing over important documents. Plus, you'll learn how to pare down your filing system so the stack of paid bills waiting to be filed does not pile up.

Before we get into the tips for your finances, I want to be sure you have a simple system for dealing with your monthly bills. You are going to need a home for the bills, both the incoming ones and the ones to be mailed. Three ideas are a basket with two distinct internal compartments, a two compartment vertical sorter, or a plastic caddy with a left and a right side and a center handle. Place the items commonly used while paying bills, like stamps, return address labels, a calculator, your checkbook, a pen, and a pencil in the bill container. You will also need a system for the paid bills, try using a twelve-slot accordion folder labeled by category, utilities, insurance, car, home, and so on. Keep the accordion file for the year, and file it away with your taxes at the end of the year. Once you have the items you need, it will take less than an hour to set up this system. Set aside the time and do it this week.

Your new routine will be to open the bills as they come in. Keep only the bill and return envelope, unless you pay online, in which case you can toss the envelope as well. Place the bills in the unpaid side of the bill-paying container. During your bill-paying session, check the receipts against your credit card statement and the debits against your bank statement.

Next, pay the bills. Be sure to put the ones you need to mail out in your "in/out" tote bag or near the front door so you can grab them on your way out. Place the stubs from the paid bills on the paid side of the caddy. At the end of the month, once everything has been paid, stick all the stubs in the twelve-pocket accordion file. At the end of the year, simply file it away with your tax return as back up documentation in the event you ever need it. With this foolproof system for bill paying you will not incur any more late fees due to disorganization. Now let's get to work on those other financial papers.

37.

Simplify Your Financial Record Keeping

841. Pare down what you get in the first place. Opt for email statements if possible.

842. Direct any online statements directly to a folder in your email inbox. That way they do not clog up your basic inbox.

843. Block off a small chunk of time monthly on your calendar to deal with financial paper and records. About one hour a week or two hours biweekly is realistic.

844. During this chunk of time, balance your checkbook(s). This task has been made super easy with the ability to access your real-time bank statement online or by phone. You will know what is pending and what has cleared. A simple comparison between the bank's records and your own will get your account up to date.

845. If you have a gift certificate that is about to expire, but you are not ready to use it yet, just go buy another gift certificate using the money from the one you already have.

846. Keep your most recent statement and permanently store the year-end statement. Since you can now print a statement directly from your bank online, you do not have to keep every paper one.

847. Keep years together. Change your check register on December 31st so you can file it with that year's papers.

848. Write a master list of bills with the contact information for the payees. Keep this list in your disaster-proof box for use in the event of an emergency.

38.

Bill Paying Made Easy

849. Change the billing due dates to the same day of the month. That way you can pay bills one time a month. If your creditors will not change the date then simply pretend that they did and pay early.

850. Consider an auto payment option using a credit card or bank draft.

851. Try online bill pay. Many banks offer the option at no additional change. It will save you time, stamps, and envelopes. Many banks offer the option to schedule a future payment, so you can log on one time a month and schedule your bills to be paid.

852. You might choose to use a bill sorter. It is a box with thirty-one slots in it. The way to use it is to slip each bill into the number slot of the day it is due as soon as it arrives. When you do pay bills pick everything out of the slots between then and the next time you will be paying bills. If you prefer not to mail the checks immediately, you can slip the bill ready to be mailed in the date to mail it, then check the box periodically and mail the ones ready to go.

853. Place items waiting for payment, including charitable donation requests and other items that need a check like things for the children such as sports uniform orders and class trips, in the bill paying caddy or the "to be paid" slot of your bill organizer. Before you do that, make sure to note it on the calendar, this ensures you'll pay on time and not incur those inflated late fees.

854. In your desktop file box, you can have two files for bills, ones to be paid on the fifteenth of the month, and ones to be paid on the thirtieth of the month.

855. Use a thirteen-slot accordion folder for filing your paid bills. Slide in the preprinted monthly tabs and write the year on the front of the file. Then as you pay bills simply place the stub in the slot of the month you paid it. At the end of the year tie up the file, store it with the taxes and start a new one.

856. An alternative is an A–Z slotted accordion folder. File by company name for one year then wrap it up and store it at year end.

TOSS

No-brainer toss list: Stubs from bills paid that you do not need to retain for tax purposes, the inserts that come in with the bills and any old organizers that you tried but did not work for you.

Part Eleven:

Family Clutter

Family—love them, don't always love all their stuff. Children have a lot of stuff: toys, papers, and articles of clothing just to name a few. Sometimes, it can feel like all you do is clean up after them. Add to that all their activities, art projects, and invitations to birthday parties, and you have a full-time job right there. Add to that a partner who shares your space but may not have the same style of organization as you. All this is enough to leave you frazzled and feeling overwhelmed.

However, you'll be glad to know that there are some creative and fun ways to get everyone involved in organizing the home and keeping it that way. Here are the very best tips to help you and your family sort out the stuff, put it away, and keep it that way, without nagging or ultimatums.

39.
Children

857. Involve your children in the organizing process: hide coins among the items to be put away which they can keep as they find them; play music from their favorite CD, set a timer and when it goes off they are done; label the shelves, bins, and baskets; be specific (instead of "Clean your room," say, "Put all the board games away and make your bed. Put all the books back on the shelf."); and write out and post instructions to some of the tasks like sorting laundry.

858. Help children learn to purge. Ask them to locate three stuffed toys and one board game for donation. Be specific in your direction. You might also help them give away some of their best artwork by mailing it to family members.

859. Show children the cost of time. Tell them that if they help you with X, then they can have what they are asking for—like playing a card game with you.

860. Help build their confidence. Resist the urge to redo their work. It may not be done your way but it is done. This makes them feel good about the task they have completed.

861. Learn to delegate by setting up a chore chart. Children can help you cook, and while they help they can be learning math skills as you quiz them about measurements. Or, they can help with the laundry as they learn to sort and read directions. Create a list of the chores that need to be done around the house. Then ask everyone in the house to sign up for a specific number of chores each. By allowing them to choose, they are more willing to pitch in.

BONUS TIP FOR LONG TERM SUCCESS:

Ask the child to also list the repercussion for not doing the chore. Their punishment will usually be harsher then something you would have chosen.

862. Chore rotation. Use this technique to avoid being called unfair because it is perceived you ask one child to help more often. This also clears your mind of trying to remember who just helped. You can make the process argument free by writing one child's name per day on the calendar. If you have three children, the oldest one's name is written on the first day of the month, the middle child on day two and the youngest on day three. Then repeat the sequence all the way through the month. Then on any given day you can call on that child to be the special helper.

863. To avoid the chore routine becoming boring, have everyone pick new chores to do often. In addition, if on a particular night someone wants to switch, make a special allowance.

864. Instead of asking the children to make their beds or hang up coats, give the mundane tasks fun names. So, instead of nagging them to place their dishes in the sink you can say "water guns" and allow them to use the spray nozzle to wash the food from their plates.

865. Check in with your children officially every week or two to ask how things are going. This is a great time to relate new house rules, divvy up new chores, and so on.

866. Checklists are a great way for every member of the family to be reminded of routine tasks. As a fun craft project at home, you can create checklists with each child for them to use daily. The checklists can hang on a bedroom doorknob, behind a door, or in the bathroom. List all the tasks and chores to be done on specific days. For example, if Monday is library day, then a check box for that day means to pack the library book. If Tuesday is laundry day, they might be responsible for bringing their dirty clothing to the laundry room. The checklist can also show daily tasks such as brushing teeth, combing hair, and so on. For younger children, a short checklist with two or three pictures works well to start the habit early.

867. Designate one bin, basket, or container as the homework caddy. Give each child his or her own. In the caddy, keep all the supplies that are commonly required to do a homework project—for young children, crayons, scissors, glue, and markers. Store them near the homework area with extra supplies nearby so the caddies can easily be refilled.

BONUS TIP:
The homework caddy can travel with you. When you are waiting for one child to finish an extracurricular activity, another one can be working on a project.

868. When crayons, pencils, and sidewalk chalk are used up to a one-inch nub, toss them.

869. If you have more than one child to help get ready in the morning, try staggering their wake up times. Wake one child up, and then wait ten or fifteen minutes before waking up the other. This gives you and the first child time to do tasks without interruptions; plus, if bathroom space is an issue, one child can go in at a time.

870. Try this new family rule: No television in the morning until you are all ready to go.

871. Help children build confidence around parting with items. Ask them to locate five toys to donate, help them choose one of three art projects they created to recycle, or help them give away clothing they will not wear. The more you do it the easier it gets.

872. Pull the plaques off trophies and keep them instead of keeping entire trophies.

873. For easier access to closets, take off the doors. You can opt to leave the doors off and use decorative containers in the closet. Or, you can hang a tension shower curtain rod with a curtain.

874. If you find the papers coming home from school are often lost or sit in cluttered piles try an inbox. Appoint one area as the inbox; it can be a desk tray, a basket, a drawer, or your choice. As soon as your children come home from school, their first stop should be the inbox where they dump all the papers to be reviewed. You can then sort through them when you have a moment, deciding what is a nice project to compliment them on, what is a test to be reviewed, and what is an urgent notice that needs action. To ensure success, the inbox must be gone through daily by an adult.

875. These days, children seem to be invited to a record number of birthday parties. And if you have more than one child, the invitations can be even more difficult to track. To help keep the invites under control follow these steps: as soon as an invitation arrives check your calendar to see if that date and time are open, if they are not, you can decline immediately. If the date is open, then ask your child if they wish to attend; if so, the RSVP needs to be made. (At the appropriate age, it is a good skill for children to practice; they can call with your assistance.) Immediately mark the event on the calendar; then count back to the weekend before the event and mark the calendar to remind yourself a gift and card need to be purchased. Place the actual invitation in a file labeled party invites. When the party date arrives, you can easily put your fingers on the invitation so you know who, what, where, and when.

BONUS TIP:
Try to arrange car pool ahead of time so you only have to drive one way.

876. Stop the insane weekends of running from one event to another and not enjoying any of them. Make a decision about how many events each person is going to attend and stick to that number. Six weekend events a month is a realistic goal. Two events per weekend, with one weekend free. Anything over that and you either have to decline or swap events.

877.
Throughout the year, you may have ideas for fun party themes or venues for your children's events. The key is to remember them as the special day draws near. There are two great ways to collect these ideas. You can either jot down your thoughts on the calendar on the date of the child's special day or you can start a folder clearly labeled "party ideas" where you can place cool invitations you receive to use as inspiration, newspaper clippings of party places, and all the other thoughts that come to mind.

BONUS TIP:
Use this folder during the actual planning phase as well, so you have one place to look for the invitation list and other related paperwork.

878.
Online invitations are becoming increasingly popular. Within minutes, you can have your invitations sent and save the postage. Websites such as www.evite.com allow you to choose from thousands of themed invitations and personalize them. You can opt to have an email sent to you as your guests reply. You can tailor the invitation by adding a note or a map, asking guests to bring something and so much more. The sites are so user friendly you do not have to be a computer whiz to create your invitation.

879. A meaningful way of saying thank you for a gift your child received is to take a picture of your child using the gift, either holding it, playing with it, or wearing it, whatever the case may be. Send the photo in the thank-you card—this personal touch is appreciated.

880. When your child has a party, the added chore of having to write out a ton of thank-you notes can feel overwhelming. A great tip is to be sure to get a group shot of the attendees during the party. Then have that picture developed and use the photo as your thank you card. Get 4 x 6 copies made, write your note of thanks on the left hand side of the back, saving room for the mailing address on the right hand side. Stick on the postage and you are all set.

881. If you have ever felt bad about the fact that the thank-you notes went out weeks or even months after the gift was received (or sometimes not at all) you can create a new household rule. The thank-you note must be written and mailed before the gift can be opened and used or the money can be spent or deposited.

882. Instead of staring at a pile of notes to be written and feeling so over-whelmed that you don't write any of them, write a few every night until they are all done.

883. If your child takes part in activities, usually you receive a schedule of events. To easily organize the schedules you can take a few minutes and transfer the information onto one family calendar then post the schedule page in the child's room so they can review it themselves.

884. You can also place all the current schedules into a file labeled event schedules. Then the next time you need one it will be at your fingertips. When filing papers you need on a daily or weekly basis you can group them by category, such as event schedules, or by person such as "Erik's schedules."

885. To allow your children to more fully enjoy the activities they are interested in try setting a limit about how many events they will sign up for each season. One indoor and one outdoor activity per season is usually a realistic guideline. Anything over that and you should either decline or swap activities.

886. For each activity and grade in school children often receive a roster or a phone list of everyone in the group. Keeping all of them grouped together in a file near your phone book is a great way to organize them for speedy reference.

When a new roster for the same person or event comes in, toss out the old one, keeping only the newest one.

887. A duplicate gift and clothes that do not fit are lost money if they are not returned in a timely manner. However having the item and the receipt with you before the return deadline can sometimes be challenging. By deciding on one place to keep all the receipts of the pending items, you can easily locate what you need. Keep items to be returned in a nearby spot as well. New household rule: In this house, we make returns on the second weekend of the month.

888. Whenever you come across an item in the house and cannot identify what or who it belongs to, simply toss it into a designated lost-and-found basket. Then when you are asked if you know where the previously unidentified item is you can direct the owner to the basket.

BONUS TIP:
If you're not a basket person, use a drawer instead.

889. The unclaimed box is a great holding spot for items not picked up after you've asked for a cleanup. Anything left out can be considered fair game and placed in an unclaimed bin. You might even choose to hold these items for ransom—to free his or her toy the child may have to help with a chore. New household rule: In our house, anything left in the unclaimed box past thirty days is donated.

890. Give each child a crate, with file rails, for all the papers they bring home. Use box bottom hanging folders (so they hold more) and label each with broad categories such as projects, study papers, artwork, each class, and so on. Then show the child how to file papers for reference throughout the school year. At the end of the school year weed the crate and save only the treasures.

891. A child who is not in school yet but does attend day care should get a crate too. File things like daily reports, class lists, health records, and permission slips in the crate by using hanging folders not manila file folders, which can be harder to access.

892. Give each child a memory box, clearly labeled with his or her name, to keep the one-of-a-kind pieces of artwork, a blanket they loved as a baby, or their first pair of shoes. It can be a plastic tub or something more decorative like a chest or a trunk. Use it to store all the items that you do not want to part with but that do not need to be displayed.

893. If an item is too large to fit in the memory box, consider taking a photo of it, adding the photo to the box and letting the actual item go.

894. Have your children help determine what makes the cut and is placed in the memory box. Decision-making skills are important at helping keep clutter at bay, and this is a great way to start.

895. To avoid impending household accidents, such as tripping and falling down the stairs, you can give each child a corner of one stair. When that portion of the stair is full then they are responsible to bring up the items and put them away. It will also help them see what belongs to them so they can get in the habit of taking the item(s) up each time they go. Ensure success: Avoid using baskets created to perch on steps. They are just clutter catchers.

896. To avoid the pass-along trap of planning to give clothing to friends or family the next time you see them, you may want to have an open house. Lay out all the items that are no longer used by your children, invite everyone over, give them a bag, and let them "go shopping." Anything not selected by the end of the day gets given away to charity.

BONUS TIP:
You can schedule a charity truck pickup for the day after the event so items do not linger in your home.

897. Each season brings with it the need for different accessories—gloves, mittens, and scarves in the winter; sunglasses, hats, sunscreen, in the summer, and so on. Hang a plastic shoe holder over the back of a door, low enough for little hands to reach, and then fill it with the season's items. At the end of the season, roll it up and store it away; then put a new one up for the new season. At the end of the two seasons you'll have what you need without wasting time filling and unfilling the pockets.

898. Gloves and mittens are commonly misplaced or missing their mate. You might try placing a string through the sleeves of the jacket and attaching one mitten or glove to each side. That way they will never be separated or lost.

899. If you've ever run around looking for the dance outfit ten minutes before practice or sent out a search party for the swim goggles just before you have to leave, you know how time-consuming and frustrating this can be. Try containing all the items relating to one activity in one spot or in one clearly-labeled bag. Then simply grab the bag and go.

900. You might also try hanging up a day-of-the-week organizer which hangs over the rod in a closet attached by a piece of Velcro and provides five large cubbies. Place items needed for each day directly in the cubby. Library books on library day, dance outfits, swim goggles, scouting uniforms, and more on the days they are needed.

901. Play dates are fun for the kids, but sometimes for you they can feel like they are more trouble then they are worth. Toys spilled out all over after a play date is done can resemble a tornado's aftermath. By taking a moment to plan a craft or activity to be done during the visit and stating the house rules upfront, you can avoid feeling crazed after a play date is over.

BONUS TIP:
Give the children a warning ten minutes before the play date will end to allow them time to clean up.

902. To put an end to the endless search for book bags and the constant reminders to pick them up so no one trips, you can simply give the book bag a home. You'll want to choose a spot that is easy for your child to reach. Make it a location that makes sense. Asking them to take it to their bedroom might not be the best idea if you want them to unpack it in the kitchen where they typically do their homework.

903. If you are short on space for the bulky book bag, you may decide to place a bench with a lift-up seat for storage near your entryway. Or you can place sturdy hooks inside a hall closet. Another option is to purchase an actual locker or cubby system with a hook for back bags and jackets as well as a shelf and a shoe rack.

904. Keeping track of school projects is a two-step process. First, place any unfinished schoolwork in a folder labeled with the child's name next to the heading "pending schoolwork" or whatever title works for you. Then, on the calendar, jot down the name of the project on the day it is due.

905. If you've ever stayed up late helping your child create a poster board project or a diorama, you are not the only one. A lack of planning will quickly lead to late-night marathon sessions. To avoid this last-minute crunch, you can prepare in advance. When your child is notified of a project's due date, note the date on the calendar; then work backwards, placing interim deadlines on smaller tasks. For example, if an undersea diorama is due on the tenth, note that on the calendar. Then work backwards, choosing a day to pick out the shoebox and find the figures. Then pick a day to create it. This also allows you a buffer period in case things do not go as planned.

906. Making a special trip to the store to spend money on little plastic animals to fit in a diorama is a waste of valuable time. Section off a part of a shelf to collect miscellaneous items as you come across them. A box to contain all the little animals and figures is a great way to have them handy when needed.

907. Place all the items you need for a specific project in one caddy. Then carry the caddy to where you are going to work. It saves time since you have everything you need at hand and cleanup is a snap.

908. Keep poster board, shoeboxes, felt bits, feathers, buttons, and other commonly called for materials to complete projects in a school project box. This will help you avoid the dash to the store for an item the night before a project is due.

909. A great technique for handling papers that require immediate attention is to have a single clip stuck in a prominent place. A magnetic clip on the refrigerator works well. This is where papers like permission slips which need to be signed and retuned the next day can be placed until you make the time to deal with them. The key is to be sure the clip is empty before you go to bed each night.

910. The "sign and send back" clip also works well for tests or homework that needs a parent's look over and signature.

911. Make it easy for kids to do. Make sure hooks are hung low enough to reach and bins are not filled so full that they are too heavy to move.

912. Be very clear when giving your child instructions about new rules or helping around the house and ask your child to repeat back to you what they are to do. This way you can catch any miscommunication that might have occurred.

913. Reward successes with fun projects and time spent how the child wants.

914. Try your best to compliment a job well done and not to criticize unless it is important to correct the mistake.

915. Make shopping for school clothes and supplies an event by going twice a year and making a day of it.

916. When you pick your child up from a birthday party go through their goodie bag with them. Put food items in the kitchen and take the other items out of the bag right away. Designate one drawer, container, or bin for all the little items that get collected, like fast food restaurant toys, cereal box prizes, and goodie bag fillers. When the goodie bin is full, it is time to purge.

917. Musical instruments are usually expensive, are sometimes accompanied by many spare pieces, and definitely need a home of their own. If you have many instruments, you may choose to have a musical closet. A shelf or a section of an entertainment center works equally well. Instruments are to be retuned there when not in use. And if they need to be taken to school make a note on the calendar or add it to the child's checklist.

918. Whether you pack a lunch or hand out lunch tickets or lunch money, there is a simple way to be sure you are not running to school to drop off food. Pack lunches the night before or hand out the tickets or money as book bags are being packed. Add lunch to the child's morning checklist.

919. Lunch tickets can be put in a decorative cookie jar on the counter or kept in an envelope or file folder. Whatever the system, be consistent. You don't want to look in three or four places only to find out they are not there.

920. If you need small bills for lunch money, make it a habit to go to the bank and keep an envelope of small bills specifically for lunch.

921. Store toys where they are used. Some toys are quiet toys and perfect for the living room; others, like arts and crafts supplies are better left in the kitchen. Separate toys into categories according to where your kids are allowed to play with them and store them close by.

922. If you have shower doors or prefer not to have the tub toys out in plain sight then install a tension pole with baskets in one corner of the tub, this will allow you to store lots of toys within easy reach.

923. If your child enjoys being read a story while in the tub, you may find it convenient to store a few books in the bathroom as well.

BONUS TIP:
Tape yourself reading your child a bedtime story. Play it while they are in the bath, on a busy night, or when you are not home.

924. Be sure to ask your children how they like to group and store the toys. They may prefer to play with the toy cars and the blocks at the same time. That means that storing them near each other or together makes the most sense. You may not have thought of it that way and that is why asking them is vital to the success of the organizing system.

925. Dress-up clothes can be stored in a large chest or trunk. Hang dress-up hats on hooks placed on the wall. Consider a plastic shoe holder attached to the back of the door where dress-up accessories, including shoes, can be tucked away.

926. Remember in school when the bell would sound five minutes before the end of class signaling teachers and students to cleanup? Well it worked, and it can work in your home too. Set a timer to ring five minutes before you need to leave the house. Everyone will soon be in the habit of cleaning up and putting their coats on to avoid the last minute mad dash.

927. Often children have much more than they can actually use or play with at one time, which is one of the biggest causes of clutter. To help trim the toys, clothes, and books without tossing any out you can rotate. Gather up the toys, books, and out of season clothing. Group it by type and clearly label it; then store it away. Mark the date on your calendar when you would like to remind yourself that it is time to rotate. Lastly, if the item is not missed you may reconsider donating it to someone with fewer toys, clothes, or books than you own. (Be sure to let your kids know when you're rotating or donating, so it won't come as an unpleasant surprise the next time they're looking for a particular toy.)

928.

Diaper bags can easily be organized by using smaller bags inside a larger bag. For example, use one smaller bag with toys, one for cleanups, and so on. Then when packing the large bag fill it with the smaller bags that you might need. Color code or label the smaller bags so you can pack the ones you need without stopping to look inside them. Another option is to use the removable organizer that is on the market. This item has many handy pockets and can be inserted into any bag or purse where it will line the walls. Then if you want to switch bags simply take the entire piece out and insert it into another bag.

TOSS

No-brainer toss list: Books that are too torn to read, artwork that does not hold much meaning, papers from past school years, and toys that are below his or her skill level.

40.

Partner

929. The first step in conquering clutter with your partner is to team up with that person. There can be no blame. There is clutter to be dealt with and for it to work you need to do it together, no matter where it came from or why it is still there. It can't be one person's responsibility.

930. Take a photo of the area and view it together. Seeing the clutter in a picture makes it more real. When you live with the clutter, it can just become part of the landscape and you can become oblivious to it. However, when seeing it in the picture, there is no denying it.

931. It makes it much easier for your partner if he or she understands how the clutter makes you feel. By telling them what bothers you and why, it helps the other person see that there are emotions tied up in the clutter. They may just be seeing the stuff and not realize it has a deep effect.

932. Talk about the effects of clutter, again without blame. Are bills paid late and late fees assessed? Is there lost intimacy in your relationship because of the clutter? Are your lives more stressful because you can't find things? Would you entertain more if you didn't have to clean so much? Does your budget suffer because you rebuy items you already own and can't find?

933. Make a promise to the other person that neither one of you will make decisions about or clear out the other person's stuff without permission.

934. Also promise each other that once you choose to let something go there is no more debate about it. Also, there will be no going through bags of items to bring something back into the house.

935. One of the easiest starting places is to find common ground. Pick an area that the both of you can work on. Choose something small and visible: a countertop, a floor, entryway, or other space. Then, craft a plan of attack. Dive in together to clear the area.

936. Talk about your definition of clutter with each other. Also discuss what makes an area clutter-free. You may have two different opinions of when an area is clutter-free, and it will be important to compromise.

937. Try not to choose an area to begin with that is highly emotional. Clothing, books, and other treasures are tough to begin with because there are too many decisions, and it can be challenging to part with these things. Old coupons and dead batteries in a junk drawer might be just the place to get your feet wet.

938. Sometimes it is easier to part with things if you know they are going to a good home to be used. Often it is as simple as finding a charity; once you've done that, your partner may be more willing to let stuff go.

939. To make the decluttering process run as smoothly as possible and to minimize the risk of hurt feelings set up some guidelines ahead of time. No name-calling. If things get heated, take a break. No tossing out the other person's stuff. If you can't decide on an item put it to the side and move on. These are all examples of guidelines you can have in place before you set out to work together.

940. A reward can be a great motivator. Each of you should write out a list of things you'd like. Then as you hit milestones in the clutter-clearing process, no matter how big or small, you can choose a reward and treat yourself for a job well done.

941. Stop just dumping stuff around the house. Don't buy anything else until you've organized what you already own.

942. Accept the fact that we can't change people.

943. If you've been demanding that an area be cleaned up and so far it has not been, you might consider changing the way you ask. Instead of demanding, you might try negotiating.

944. Sometimes you can designate the living area of the home a clutter-free zone but allow your partner to have a specific area in the home where they can store whatever they want to without your comment.

945. Check in often with the person who has to make the decisions about their stuff. It can be difficult to make a choice to part with things, so ask if there is anything you can do to make the process easier.

946. Accept a task well done, even if it is not done exactly how you would have done it. Be open to the possibility that someone else may have another way of doing something and that it may actually work out as well or better than how you had been doing it.

947. Sometimes simply lowering your standards for a clutter-free home can be helpful. *Perfect* is a high standard to meet; maybe the both of you would be happier with just *good*.

948. Be sure to acknowledge progress. Do it in a way that is very positive. Do not compliment and then take it away by adding a statement like "but there is still more on the floor." Instead, simply offer the compliment and leave it at that. Later, if you must, offer the critique in a delicate way.

949. Many times, if you start to sort through your own belongings, the clean sweep is contagious and other family members will sort and purge as well.

950. Take turns. You let something go and then it is the other person's turn to let something go and so on and so on.

951. Before you get started, have all the tools you will need. Make the process as easy as possible by having boxes for charitable donations and bags for garbage ready to go.

952. Make the process as fun as possible. Play music, have snacks, or set a timer and race each other to see who can sort through more stuff before the bell goes off.

953. Divvy up the tasks and make a list of who is in charge of what. You might choose to have one person in charge of the inside living area and the other person to be in charge of the outside and the storage areas. Or you can divvy up specific tasks like recycling and vacuuming. This way the work is split and no one person feels like they are putting out more effort.

954. If you want, you can make the clutter-clearing effort competitive. Each of you picks something that belongs to the other person. Then once an area is deemed clutter-free the first person to make it messy gives up their item to charity.

955. Once an area is clutter-free, take a photo of it. You might even post the photo as a reminder of all your hard work and motivation to maintain the room's clutter-free status.

956. Share your decluttering mission with friends and family. Ask them to support you by not buying or bringing you anything until you are done. And ask them to gently remind you of your mission if you are out together and you start to slide back into old patterns.

BONUS TIP:

If you would usually go to garage sales with friends or family, ask them not to invite you to sales. Instead you can fill that time by doing something else or helping each other get organized.

957. Ask friends and family to keep great bargains and deals to themselves. At this point you do not need to be told about two-for-one sales.

958. If you have family and friends who bring you items that they have found while decluttering their own homes, ask them to stop.

FAST

Get started fast by picking a small area to start with and put a goal date on the calendar to have the area completed by. Block off time on the calendar before the goal date to work on the area.

Part Twelve:

Maintaining All Your Hard Work

Once you have an area clutter-free, your mission is to keep it that way. Some days it may feel like you are fighting a losing battle and that's okay. Days like that will be fewer and fewer as time goes by. But once in awhile they will creep up on you. The key is to make sure they don't overwhelm you and just get back on track. On other days, keeping an area clear will just happen naturally because you've changed old habits. Once cleared, an area must stay that way no matter what. Every person in the household has to be on board with that decision or you'll be back at square one in the blink of an eye.

The easiest way to maintain all that you've accomplished is to commit to a few guidelines that will work for you and your household. You might even want to have a fun family word that can be used if someone in the house catches another family member putting something down where it doesn't belong. This adds fun and an air of playfulness to the process.

Take a moment now and pick the new guidelines for your household that when followed consistently will keep the clutter at bay.

41.

Break Old Patterns with These New Rules

959. Use the Novak Method. Give everything a home, and after using an item, put it back where it belongs before you move on to another project, no matter what.

960. Like with like. Keep this simple rule in mind and house the similar items together. That way you will never have unrelated items mixed. It is hard to locate batteries when they are tossed behind boxes of cereal in the pantry.

961. One in, one out. This rule works especially well with children since they are more agreeable to let an older less-used toy go to charity when they have a brand new toy to play with.

962. Everything gets a home. Make sure that as new items come into your home they are given a designated place to be stored. A common setback happens after a holiday when many new items now need a home. Give everything a home that is both easy to remember and easy to get to. Store it where you use it.

963. Ask for consumable gifts. The less stuff you have the less you will have to worry about. So, instead of another teapot for your collection or some other gift, suggest that you'd like tickets to a play, a day at the spa, or a nice dinner out.

964. Leave room to grow. Be sure to leave enough space to store more things as you accumulate them.

965. When in doubt, throw it out. Repeat this to yourself whenever you find yourself tempted to hold onto something just in case it might be handy one day.

966. Set par levels. Decide ahead of time how many of what you will hold onto. How many plastic shopping bags will you keep? How many pairs of shoes will you own?

967. Give items expiration dates. Decide ahead of time how long you will hold onto things. How long will you keep an outfit if it does not fit? How long will you keep a magazine if it has not been read?

968. Use the two-minute rule. Commit the phrase "Two or fewer, be a doer" to memory. If a task will take you two minutes or less to complete, do it right then.

969. Eighteen item toss. On the first day of every month, make it a rule to find eighteen items you can toss by donating to charity or throwing away.

970. Eighteen-minute blocks of time. Remember to break up large tasks into smaller more doable ones.

971. Schedule organizing sessions. Make clearing clutter a regular part of your week. Pick a day and work on a project for a block of time, just as you would any other household chore.

972. Box, date, tape, and toss. Remember to use the box it, date it, tape it, and toss it trick. This works when you still have a little reservation about getting rid of some belongings. Take the items and place them in a box. List the contents on the outside of the box. Tape the box shut and place a future date on it when you'd feel more comfortable letting the items go. When the date rolls around and you have not needed to go to the box yet, then you can feel secure letting the box go. The key is to not open the box when the date comes up. If you do, you will just be reminded of all the reasons why you thought you could not let go of the items in the first place.

973. Ask before you buy. Before you buy something new, ask yourself, "Where will I put this?" If you have a good answer, then buy it. If not, write it down and go back to buy it later if you decide to make room for it.

974. Sixty seconds. If you have to think about keeping an item for a minute or longer, then it is probably not worth keeping.

975. Buy low-maintenance items. Watch how much maintenance the items you buy will need. Hand-wash-only garments, toys with many little pieces to keep track of, and little figurines that require dusting may not be the wisest choices.

976. Consider it clutterproofed. Once you have gone through the trouble of clearing an area, keep it that way by simply deciding that the area is clutterproofed. No one is to drop anything there, anytime, for any reason.

BONUS TIP:
If you need to, post a sign there until it becomes a habit. Or place something decorative in the space so it is not an open area tempting you to place something there.

977. Consistency is the key. Keep up your clutter-clearing habits, but allow for times when things might slide back a little. When you are not feeling well, during the holidays, and other busy times during the year, you might slip a little. It's all right, just jump right back in as soon as things calm down a bit.

978. Give a clean up warning. Remember to give everyone, including you, a fair warning before it is time to leave. That gives everyone time to put things away and get ready to leave.

979. Wrap a new habit. When you take on a new habit, try wrapping it around an already existing one. You are more likely to have success by doing it that way. For example, if you plug your shredder in by the washing machine, then every time you put in a load of laundry you could shred a pile of paperwork containing sensitive papers, that way you will be less apt to forget or skip it.

980. Give yourself twenty-eight days. Remember, it takes about twenty-eight days to create a new habit. So, if you find yourself starting a new one, then the habit drops off, simply start again and give yourself a month to instill the new habit.

981. Be positive. It's easy to look at all there is left to do. Instead, focus on what you did accomplish. At the end of the day, count the successes; no matter how small you think they are, they all count.

982. Bag it. Be sure to take everything out of its bag immediately. Do not leave anything in a bag once you come home.

983. Put it away. When you are finished with an item put it away immediately. You'll gain confidence every time you go to get something and it is right where it should be.

984. Expect setbacks. It is possible that from time to time you will slip back into old patterns. If that happens, roll with it. Just start again.

985. Maintain. Be sure to only put what belongs there in a particular spot. If you let the rule slide and start to mix things, then it becomes easier to let other areas slide as well.

986. Pass it along. If you find something that you think you could pass along to someone, you must have someone specific in mind. If not, give it to charity instead. Otherwise you run the risk of holding onto lots of things with no real plan about how to get rid of them.

987. Gauges. Remember an organized room takes no more than five minutes to clean up, and when you are organized, you can find an item in sixty seconds or less. If this stops being the case, reassess the space to be sure it remains clutter-free.

988. Family meetings. Continue to hold family meetings to check in with each other about how things are going, to brainstorm solutions to problems, and to keep the lines of communication open.

989. Use it or lose it. Decide that if you are not using something, you are going to pass it along to someone who will.

990. The moving test. Give it the moving test—if you were moving would you go through the trouble of taking it with you? If not, reconsider your decision to hold onto it.

991. Give fair warning. While you are clutterproofing, hang a sign that reads, "Please do not disturb. Clutter-clearing session in progress." It will help remind you to stay focused and will let others know you are working and should not be interrupted until the timer rings.

992. Once you have decluttered an area, you can declare it clutterproofed. Place a sign there that reads, "Clutterproofed area. Do not leave anything here." to help everyone remember not to drop things in the space. Either hang the sign on the doorknob of the room or lay the sign on the space as a gentle reminder for a few days.

FAST

Get started fast by choosing three habits to help maintain your clutter free area and put them into place immediately. Add in new habits slowly, waiting a week or two for them to solidify before adding another.

Part Thirteen:

Success Is Just a Step Away

Let's face it, clearing-clutter can be hard work. And keeping areas clutterproofed can be even more challenging. Sometimes we just don't want to go through the mail or pick up one more stranded toy or wash another load of laundry. Don't let the hard work frighten you. Most of the things in life worth going after take a little work. Nevertheless, the reward and sense of accomplishment are worth it.

It all begins with getting over the first hurdle. To do that, you simply have to do something. There are no two ways about it. Here are some helpful tidbits to help you get and stay on track.

993. Whether you believe it or not right now, you already possess everything you need to have the clutter-free home you want. It's what you do with the information that counts.

994. Remind yourself why you want to tackle the clutter. Everyone has their own reasons and some are very personal. Knowing why will help keep you going.

995. Remember the simple fact that you get more out of life when you own less. Own less and live more, it is that easy.

996. Start to become more comfortable with having empty space around you. If you are not used to it then it can be a little disconcerting in the beginning.

997. Setbacks are normal. Knowing that they will happen will allow you to get right back up and start again. If you are blindsided by a setback and it feels like a failure then you may be less likely to try again.

998. Focus on progress not perfection. Repeat this to yourself often.

999. Being organized is a process not a destination. There will always be more stuff requiring your attention. The inbox to life is never empty.

1000. Find a clutterproofing phrase that suits you and repeat it often. Here are a few suggestions: "I only keep what is useful," "I only hold onto what I use and love," "When I am in doubt I throw it out," "I store memories in my mind. They are not in the stuff I own." Let your mantra guide the process and watch amazing results unfold.

FAST
Get started fast by just moving one thing. Big or small, just do something now. It will start the ball rolling in the right direction.

Part Fourteen:

Simple Sevens for Success

Here is a collection of super ideas to jumpstart your clutterproofing. I know you will find yourself referring back to these often.

7 OF JAMIE'S FAVORITE CLUTTERPROOFING TOOLS

1. In/Out tote bag
2. Desktop file box and other caddies
3. Dymo Letratag label maker
4. Double rod clothing hanger
5. Shelf extenders and dividers
6. Take-out menu binder
7. Ziploc bags

7 TYPES OF ORGANIZING PERSONALITIES

1. Organizing product and tip junkie. You collect ideas and buy tools, but never actually do the work. Your solution: stop buying and reading. Instead, set a timer for eighteen minutes and tackle a small project.

2. Last on the list. You organize everyone else in the house and your stuff is messy. Your solution: Realize that you are setting an example for everyone else, and they need to become self-sufficient. Show them how to organize on their own and spend a little more time on your own stuff.

3. The keeper. You keep everything because it means something to you; you paid good money for it; it is still good; or you might use it one day. But keeping all this stuff clutters up the space and you cannot use the stuff you do love. Your solution: Work on an area that has the least amount of emotion for you and fill one bag with things you can give to a new home where they will be used and loved.

4. The last-minute emergency. The doorbell rings and you run around the house scooping stuff up and tossing it into baskets and bags. Then, you dump the basket or bag and greet your guests. Your solution: Plan ahead by breaking up a large clutter-clearing task into small jobs. Set a timer for eighteen minutes and go to work.

5. The procrastinator. You plan to spend some time decluttering but never seem to get around to it. Or, you start, pick up an item, and then put it back down again, unsure what to do with it. Your

solution: Give yourself a set schedule by making clutter-clearing dates with yourself and writing them on the calendar. Work for a small block of time, and then give yourself a reward for a job well done. You may choose to watch a television show, have a special snack, have coffee with a friend, or relax and do nothing.

6. Driven to distraction. You set out to tackle an area and find something that belongs in another room. You bring it there, and while you are there get caught up doing something else, leaving your original project undone. Your solution: Focus on the task at hand by making a pile of items to deliver somewhere else. Once the project is completed, distribute the items.

7. Perfection. You have a vision of what the space will look like; but there is no way you can live up to your high standard, so you do nothing. Your solution: Choose one small area and work on it. Resolve to make it good and go back in your spare time to perfect it.

7 WAYS TO START SMALL WITH NO-BRAINER STUFF

1. Return borrowed items.
2. Pile everything in need of repair in one place.
3. Find fifteen things you can let go of and pass along to people who need them.
4. Take out the garbage and recycling.
5. Remove unmatched things, like single socks.
6. Pick things up off the floor.
7. Take eight items from your wardrobe that are the wrong size or season.

7 MORE WAYS TO START SMALL WITH NO-BRAINER STUFF

1. Clear the top of a surface.
2. Stack all the reading material in one place.
3. Move one big item, like the piece of exercise equipment you've been meaning to part with, the crib your child has outgrown, or a broken chair.
4. Toss anything associated with a bad memory (leg cast from an accident).
5. Toss out expired coupons and empty bags.
6. Remove purchases from the shopping bags they came home in.
7. Part with items that are stained, too broken to repair, or can't be used, like socks with holes, a pair of pants once used to paint in, or pens without ink.

7 WAYS TO OVERCOME SEPARATION ANXIETY

1. If you are able to donate it then feel secure in the knowledge that the item will be used and loved by someone else.
2. If you need to throw the item away then know that it was not worth taking up your current living space.
3. Realize that if your home is taken up with stuff from the past, you live in the past, which does not allow you to live in the present day.
4. Keep in mind that if you store lots of stuff with the idea that you will use it in the future then all that stuff keeps you from living in the present.

5. Remember, with less stuff to worry about and take care of, you can enjoy your life more fully.
6. Part with items that are less sentimental to you, growing your decluttering muscle and working up to the more challenging items.
7. Remember that stuff is not a part of you and not your life. To live fully and create new memories you must create boundaries.

7 UNIQUE WAYS TO USE AN ARMOIRE

1. As a mudroom in the entryway
2. As a craft area
3. As a home office
4. As a work and tool area
5. As a bar
6. As a gardening area
7. As a laundry station

7 SIGNS YOU MIGHT NEED TO CLEAR SOME CLUTTER

1. You need to wear a hard hat to open your closet.
2. You need to push things down in the drawer to get it open or closed.
3. You have a two car garage and no cars inside it.
4. You have to move a pile of papers before you can cook or sit at the table.
5. Your clean clothes sit in laundry baskets for days.
6. Your guest room is more like a junk room.
7. You're not sure where you left your keys or phone, and you're not sure if you mailed out your bills this month.

7 GIFT AND GREETING CARD IDEAS

1. Keep generic gifts on hand to use at the last minute. Candles, art sets, and gift certificates that do not expire are always smart choices.
2. Keep a stash of gift bags and tissue paper near the gifts.
3. Maintain a gift file that holds gift ideas including pages ripped from catalogs.
4. Start a greeting card caddy with cards for all occasions including some blank ones.
5. There is an easy way to stock the box of greeting cards. Over the next year, each time you buy a card for any occasion buy an extra one. Use one and keep the other in your box. By the end of the year, your box will be stocked with cards you selected. Otherwise, you can opt to purchase a prefilled box.
6. Paper clip greeting cards to the corresponding month on the calendar, that way you will remember to send them on time.
7. Host a re-gift party after the holidays when everyone brings gifts they were given but will not use so they can swap for something they like.

7 STEPS FOR MEASURING FOR A CUSTOM CLOSET

1. Take an inventory of the items you want to store in the closet so you know how to plan the space.
2. Measure the walls, door, and ceiling of the closet (measure three areas of the same wall, and note the smallest measurement. Often the closet is not perfectly rectangular).

3. Write down the door type (pocket, bifold, sliding, or other).
4. Note any irregularities in the closet.
5. Write down any cut outs, wires, pipes, vents, lights, and other special features.
6. Write down your height—this makes a big difference as to how high and low areas of the closet are easy for you to reach.
7. Take note of some hanging spaces typically needed in a closet. Blazers and skirts need 38-42", long shirts 36-40", long dresses and long coats 60-70", cocktail dresses and pants hung from their cuff 48-50", pants folded over the hanger 20". Placing the top clothing rod at 82" high allows room for a second rod to be installed below it.

7 SMALL SPACES IDEAS

1. Use your vertical space.
2. Multipurpose furniture. An example is an ottoman that opens for storage or a trunk or chest doubling as a coffee table.
3. Use the backs of room doors and the insides of cabinet doors.
4. Use the perimeter of the room. Install shelves eighteen inches below the ceiling on all or some of the walls.
5. Store items under the bed.
6. Hang items like pots and pans.
7. A decorator table with a floor length tablecloth disguises storage area underneath.

7 NO- OR LOW-COST ORGANIZING SOLUTIONS

1. Use a towel bar (the straight metal type meant to hold hand towels in the bathroom) as a lid rack on the inside of the kitchen cabinet for hanging pot lids of various sizes.
2. Make slip-proof hangers by sticking non-skid chair pads to them.
3. Box lids or small, metal loaf pans make great drawer dividers.
4. Use mugs to hold cotton swabs, pens, nail files, and craft brushes.
5. Baking sheets make handy shoe trays (for a disposable version, use foil baking sheets).
6. Use glass jars as organizers, tall ones for rulers, and low ones for pens.
7. Muffin pans or egg cartons can hold jewelry or office supplies in desk drawers. Use a cake decorator's icing tip to hold rings while you wash your hands.

7 THINGS TO STORE IN A THREE-RING BINDER FILLED WITH SHEET PROTECTORS

1. Printed directions from online mapping sites.
2. Recipes by category or menus from restaurants that offer take-out.
3. Warranties and instruction manuals for household items.
4. Ideas, sketches, contracts, and paperwork relating to a home remodel.
5. Bids, business cards, paperwork, and notes relating to selling your house and moving.

6. Schedules, school calendars, and phone lists for everyone in the house.
7. Newspaper and magazines clippings.

7 USES FOR A PLASTIC CADDY

1. Homework caddy
2. Cleaning caddy
3. Nail care caddy
4. Car wash caddy
5. Pet care caddy
6. Craft caddy
7. Bill paying caddy

7 WAYS TO DOWNSIZE BEFORE RELOCATING

1. Pass along heirloom pieces now so you can tell the story about them.
2. Give back items that don't belong to you to their owner.
3. Have family members take what they left behind when they moved out.
4. Pare down the quantity of the items you are keeping.
5. Limit the number of collections you own and maintain.
6. Prepare to pack and move only the items you will have a use for in your new space.
7. If you are moving to a smaller space, be mindful of the size of your current furniture.

7 MOVING TIPS

1. Create a timeline.
2. Use a three-ring binder as the moving binder where you store all the critical information.
3. Create a box of "maybe items." You'll pack and move them; but if you don't use them in the new space, you'll toss them.
4. Host a moving party. Ask guests to bring boxes and pack as you socialize.
5. Schedule a few pickups by local charities to let others benefit from what you are not going to take with you.
6. Before you pack it, ask yourself if you love it enough to move it. Be sure it fits your new life.
7. Sketch out and measure new space to see what furniture will fit before moving it.

7 MORE MOVING TIPS

1. Use up the food in the refrigerator before moving day.
2. Do not pack anything that is in need of repair or is dirty.
3. Designate one room as packing central where you store moving boxes, packing tape, and other supplies.
4. Pack up one room and set it up the same in the new space to keep some continuity as you make a change so it feels like home.
5. Place packing supplies in one caddy or in a pack that attaches to your belt. That way you'll always have a marker, scissors, and other supplies at your fingertips.
6. Choose one location to store all the paperwork,

warranties, and instruction manuals related to the new appliances in the new space.

7. Pack a few mini-boxes of the essentials including an emergency kit with Band-Aids, a flashlight, a corded phone, candles and matches, and emergency phone numbers. Then label them "open first."

7 TIPS FOR INTERVIEWING MOVERS

1. Review their insurance coverage thoroughly and ask about their claims process for damages.
2. Call their references and check the Better Business Bureau at www.bbb.org for complaints.
3. Understand the assembly and disassembly charges fully.
4. Ask what boxes and packing supplies are included.
5. Figure out how they charge—hourly or by weight.
6. Ask how they estimate the date when your boxes will arrive and what they will reimburse you if they fall behind schedule.
7. Find out what method of payment is accepted and how you make the final payment.

7 THINGS THAT BELONG IN YOUR MOVING SURVIVAL BOX

1. Bed linens
2. Towels
3. Soap
4. Paper products

5. Cleaning supplies
6. Change of clothes
7. Trash bags

7 MORE THINGS THAT BELONG IN YOUR MOVING SURVIVAL BOX

1. Coffeemaker and mugs
2. Corded phone (the battery in the cordless may need time to recharge)
3. Water and ice (pack the ice in a cooler the day of the move)
4. Eating and cooking utensils
5. Take-out menus
6. Pet food and water dish
7. Alarm clock

7 INGENIOUS IDEAS TO MAKE ORGANIZING FUN

1. Host a round robin organizing party. Start at your home and organize, then move to the next person's home.
2. Throw a photo party where everyone bring a bag of photos to put into an album.
3. Make a decluttering date and write it in pen on the calendar.
4. Have a decluttering party complete with food, music, and a prize at the end.
5. Invite others to a giving party. Have everyone bring a bag of good stuff they no longer love that they can swap for stuff they will use.
6. Barter with friends to help you with large decluttering projects or ask them to watch your

children so you can have some uninterrupted time.

7. Set up rewards for yourself. Acknowledge successes and celebrate a job well done.

7 TIPS TO HELP MAKE YOUR FAMILY STRESS-FREE

1. Set up a car pool.
2. Limit afterschool activities, like soccer and scouts, to one per child per season.
3. Schedule multiple practices at the same time if possible.
4. Block off in pen one free weekend a month.
5. Compare calendars with everyone in the house to avoid double-booking.
6. Work off one master family calendar to avoid confusion.
7. Schedule family meetings to catch up on what's been going on and to resolve issues.

7 TIPS FOR STRESS-FREE MORNINGS

1. Hang a master checklist to be sure you and everyone in the home have everything you need before you leave the house.
2. Preset the table for breakfast. For a quick and easy cleanup on rushed days use paper products.
3. Pack lunches or hand out lunch tickets the night before.
4. Be sure backpacks are packed before bedtime.
5. Give yourself enough time to wake up and get ready before the children get up.

6. Stagger the wakeup times of the children so you can devote attention to one child at a time.
7. Make it a family rule that there is no television unless there is extra time once everyone is ready to walk out the door.

7 TIPS FOR STRESS-FREE EVENINGS

1. Instead of buying take-out dinners on busy evenings, opt to cook a frozen food item or serve ready-made food from the grocery store.
2. Allow time for you and family members to transition from a busy day to a relaxed evening.
3. Opt to play relaxing music instead of turning on the television.
4. Lower the lights and light a few candles to set a relaxing mood.
5. Try starting a new tradition where you put out a platter of vegetables or cheese and crackers.
6. Be sure to reserve one evening a week free from outside activities.
7. Schedule time to work on homework.

7 PET POINTERS

1. Hang the dog leash and baggies on a hook by the door you use most often.
2. Use the time while walking a pet to listen to a book on tape.
3. Transfer pet food or bedding chips for cages into pest and water resistant plastic bins with a scoop inside.

4. For pets that require grooming or bathing you can place all the necessary supplies in one plastic caddy. Then instead of searching for everything you need to complete the job you can simply grab the single caddy and get to work.
5. Write the pet care chores on the calendar so things are not forgotten.
6. Create a cleaning caddy with supplies needed to care for the pet so they are all in one place and easy to tote around.
7. Use a basket to collect and store all the pet's toys.

7 NECESSITIES FOR PREPARING FOR EVACUATION

1. A plan for all the people and pets
2. Important papers, address book, and identification
3. Radio with batteries, cell phone, and charger
4. Map of the area and blank paper to make notes
5. Clothing, bedding, and memorabilia
6. Comfort toys and small games like a deck of cards
7. Medications, vitamins, first aid items

7 VACATION PLANNING TIPS

1. In one spiral bound notebook, collect ideas of where you want to stop and things you want to see while you are away.
2. Designate one area of your home as the packing zone—anything that needs to be packed should be put there.
3. Put a hold on mail delivery online at www.usps.com.

4. Use the day you return to catch up on mail and laundry—even if you have to tell everyone you'll be back a day later than planned.
5. Stop your newspaper delivery.
6. Put an autoresponder on your email to alert people that you are on vacation.
7. Leave your itinerary with someone you trust and can call in an emergency.

7 TIPS TO PACK A SUITCASE

1. Pack an empty tote bag to carry back souvenirs.
2. Pack an empty laundry bag to collect dirty laundry.
3. Call ahead to where you are staying to see what services and amenities they offer. If they have a hair dryer or iron, you won't have to pack one.
4. Seal things that can spill in Ziploc bags.
5. Pack essentials in the carry on in case your luggage is lost like medications, toothbrush, and a change of clothes.
6. Pack multiuse items like a pair of black pants that you can pair with a T-shirt for a casual look or with a sequin top for a dressier style.
7. Pack mini versions of items like toothpaste or use samples.

7 GENERAL PACKING TIPS

1. Pick out what you plan to pack—then put 50 percent of it back.
2. Create a master list of the items you pack and then store it in your luggage to reuse the next time you travel.

3. Tie a ribbon or a bright strand of material to your bag so it will stand out from the crowd of other suitcases.
4. Take a picture of your luggage in case it is lost. This will make it easier for airport personnel to locate it.
5. Pack half your clothing in one suitcase and half in someone else's that way if one is lost you each still have something.
6. Ask someone to check in on your home (look for broken water pipes, a back puffing oil burner, etc.) and restock the basics in your refrigerator before you come home.
7. Pack your passport, tickets, and small bills for tipping in a small bag you'll slip around your neck.

7 WAYS TO STAY ORGANIZED WHILE ON VACATION

1. Use a toiletry bag that unrolls and hangs from the back of a door to save counter space.
2. Pack a pop-up clothes hamper for dirty laundry.
3. Schedule time to set up your hotel room before you start your vacation. A little preparation saves you a lot of time looking for things.
4. Pack a spare duffel bag to carry home all the souvenirs. Write a list of who you want to buy gifts for and check them off as you buy them to avoid overbuying.
5. Schedule time to unpack once you arrive home.
6. Take five minutes before you leave your room for the day to tidy up so when you come back the room is how you want it.

7. Bring a collapsible set of shelves that hang from the rod in the closet. The extra space will be welcome.

7 TIPS FOR UNPACKING

1. Plan an extra day at the end of vacation to unpack and get back in the routine.
2. Drop off film to be developed the day after you return or send it through the mail. (Pick up the envelopes before you leave.)
3. Give out the souvenirs you picked up for friends and family.
4. Throw a party to share photos with everyone and to distribute souvenirs.
5. Immediately upon your return, put away important documents like your passport.
6. Continue your vacation even after you return; send your vacation laundry to a laundromat to have it done for you.
7. Store away the luggage as soon as it is empty.

7 GARAGE SALE TIPS

1. Plan one with the neighbors. The larger the sale, the more people you will attract. Place the larger items that are more attractive near the road to catch the eye of people driving by.
2. Put up and then take down easy-to-read signs that are protected in case it rains. Adding balloons to the sign attracts more attention. Make sure the signs are easy to read from a distance and mention a few of the sale's high-lights.

3. Consider setting items in a large box or on a table and labeling it "Any item for $1.00."
4. To entice buyers to stay around a little longer, offer or sell cookies and coffee or water.
5. Run a towel with ArmorAll or another polishing cream over plastic items to make them shine. Place new batteries in battery-operated items. Plug in electrical items and attach the instruction manual to them.
6. At a garage sale, you need to have some change on hand to start with. A good amount is two $10.00 bills, six $5.00 bills, twenty $1.00 bills, and $10.00 in assorted change. Placing the coins in a muffin tin makes it easy to grab the right change.
7. Lastly, and most importantly, schedule a charity to come pickup the unsold items to prevent them from reentering your home!

7 NEW HOUSEHOLD RULES

1. In our home, everyone puts their dirty laundry in the laundry room on laundry day and puts away his or her own clean laundry.
2. In our home, whoever finishes the roll of toilet paper puts on a new roll.
3. In our home, when we are low on a grocery item we check it off on the master grocery list.
4. In our home, whoever takes a phone message for another person agrees to place it in the designated place. Use a phone message book with carbon in it, so you'll have a back up of the information.
5. In our home, each person clears his or her own dishes from the table.

6. In our home, each person keeps his or her closets and drawers neat.
7. In our home, if we see something out of place we put it away immediately.

7 PHOTO ORGANIZING TIPS

1. Gather all your photos. This means you need to develop all outstanding rolls of film and disposable cameras.
2. Sort the photos into piles by event, person, or time period. While doing this make an additional pile of photos to pass along to other people and use the garbage can liberally for photos that are not worth keeping.
3. Store photos and negatives separately and safely way. Use acid proof boxes that are out of direct sunlight and not exposed to extreme temperatures.
4. Work in small blocks of time to sort the photos and then to put them into albums if you so choose. Do not work in marathon blocks of time. Instead, set the kitchen timer for eighteen minutes and sort a handful—some is always better than none.
5. Place a photo on a package at holiday time as a special bonus to the gift itself.
6. Share the memories. Have a photo-organizing party or send duplicate photos to family and friends. When you find a photo you want to share with someone else, make a note of who you want to send it to. That way you won't look at it later and wonder why you tucked it aside.

7. Label the spines of the photo albums. That way you know what pictures are in what album without pulling them all off the shelves.

7 DON'TS OF PHOTO ORGANIZING

1. Don't store the photos in your basement or attic.
2. Don't store them in humidity over 70 percent (they can mildew) or under 40 percent (they can become brittle).
3. Don't expose them to direct sunlight.
4. Don't place them into magnetic pages in photo albums, as the glue will ruin the photos.
5. Don't adhere photos to black photo pages. They are not acid free and can damage the photos.
6. Don't write on the back of photos with a ballpoint pen (it breaks the emulsion and can bleed through)—instead use a photo safe pen.
7. Don't take them all out and leave them in a jumbled mess; instead work in small yet consistent blocks of time to tackle the backlog.

7 WAYS TO OVERCOME PROCRASTINATION

1. Set a deadline, even if it is self-imposed. You are more likely to complete a task if you have a target date in mind. It can be fictional or you can make it more real by scheduling an event. For example, if you have been meaning to clear out the basement so you can have it remodeled, then set up an appointment with the contractor to come in a few weeks.

2. Tell people what you are doing. Having people know what you are working on will help you finish it since you may be asked about it and you'll want to report a success.
3. Break the task up into small parts. When you have smaller tasks, they seem more manageable.
4. Set a kitchen timer for eighteen minutes and dive in. This will at least get the task started.
5. Reward yourself for a job well done or for small steps along the way.
6. Work with someone who will hold you accountable, like a professional organizer or coach. When you have to report back you'll be more likely to do the project.
7. Focus on what it will feel like to be done.

7 EMERGENCY PLANNING IDEAS

1. Have a few flashlights on hand with new batteries. Use a magnet or Velcro to attach one of them to the fuse box.
2. Keep two gallons of bottled water on hand.
3. Make sure that important and irreplaceable documents are stored in a disaster-proof box.
4. Designate a family meeting place in the event family members cannot get home. You can choose a local house of worship or even a store or school.
5. Practice fire drills regularly.
6. Institute a nickname policy. Give each child a nickname or password of sorts. Then if for some reason you're unable to pick them up after school and you send someone else, that person will use the password or the nickname.

Then the child will know it's safe to go with that person.

7. Draw a map of the home and mark where the wires, fuse boxes, and shut off valves are located.

7 THINGS TO PACK IF YOU HAVE TO EVACUATE WITH A PET

1. Cans or bags of food in air tight containers
2. Can opener
3. Water and food dishes
4. Gallons of water
5. Supplies including leashes
6. ID tag on the collar or cage/crate/container
7. Pictures of pet(s)

7 CAR TIPS

1. Keep a paint brush to brush sand off feet.
2. Keep a change of clothes in the car for each family member.
3. Stock your emergency kit and check it quarterly.
4. Tuck a list of commonly called numbers in the glove compartment, including those you'd need to call in the event of an emergency.
5. Use a cargo net in the trunk to keep things from sliding all around the trunk.
6. Keep a few of your favorite take-out menus in the car to call in an order on a day you choose not to cook.
7. Keep coupons in the car with any gift certificates you may have so you are sure to have them when you get to the store.

7 TIPS FOR STRESS-FREE HOLIDAYS

1. Label the boxes of holiday decorations "1 of 7" (or however many boxes you have). That way, the following year you'll know how many you should be looking for.

2. You can have everyone bring a dish, and then you only have to make a few items. This allows people to feel included and frees up time for you.

3. Buy some Christmas cookies and only bake the unusual ones or the ones everyone loves.

4. Keep a holiday journal where you can jot down what the holidays were like, who gave and received what gifts, and what the menu was. That way, the next year, you can avoid giving the same gifts and you can review the menu to see what was popular.

5. To avoid addressing all your holiday card envelopes, print labels for them off your computer.

6. Too many people to shop for? Consider making agreements not to buy for everyone. Instead, place the names of everyone exchanging gifts into a hat and have everyone pick one. That way you don't have to buy a ton of gifts, but everyone gets something. Avoid agreeing to "only buy for the children." The children will get plenty of gifts, and adults like getting gifts too.

7. If you'd prefer to buy more than just one grab bag gift, you can set the grab bag up with two levels of gifts—one larger gift for the first person you pick and a small gift for the second name you choose.

7 MORE TIPS FOR STRESS-FREE HOLIDAYS

1. Make displaying photos easy by using holiday-themed frames, filling them with photos of the holiday, and packing them away with the holiday items so they can be used year after year. Instead of updating the photos, leave the timeline by adding more instead of refilling them.

2. Place holiday photos from your landscaper, real estate agent, and others in a magnetic photo album. A magnetic album is the type with a clear plastic sheet that peels back from the page that is covered in lines of adhesive. This is not the place for your treasured memories, but for the photos of acquaintances and their children, this is a good solution. Pack the photo album away with the holiday decorating at the end of the season.

3. Give themed gifts every year. It will save you lots of time and planning. You can give books as gifts one year, a T-shirt with jeans another year, or a fun basket of cooking supplies.

4. String a piece of ribbon along one wall or outline a doorway with the ribbon. As holiday cards arrive, take a paper clip and clip the card to the ribbon.

5. Do as much shopping online as you can. Just check out the return policy before placing your order.

6. Take one personal day off from work to shop all day. Leave the kids at home, even if you have to hire a babysitter. Shopping without kids is less stressful. If you're shopping with a friend, consider having their kids come over to your

house. Then, a babysitter can watch all the children at one house, and you can split the cost.

7. When the holidays are over, take a moment to review the season. Jot down what you regret not making the time to do. Then clip the paper to next year's calendar so next holiday's season you can make the time.

7 TIPS FOR HOLIDAY CARDS AND GIFTS

1. Wrap the gifts as soon as you buy them and put the to/from labels on immediately. This prevents having stacks of gifts to wrap at the last moment.

2. Use pack-and-send services to avoid those long post office lines during the holidays.

3. Prepare in advance so you do not end up having to ship the gifts overnight to ensure they arrive on time.

4. Designate one place in your house to be Gift Wrap Central. At this spot, keep scissors, tape, wrapping paper, boxes, gift bags, to/from tags, tissue paper, and bows and ribbons.

5. Writing out holiday cards can be another daunting task that ends up feeling more like a chore then a warm holiday greeting. Consider typing up a family newsletter or a letter to family and friends to enclose in a card or send with one. You can update people on what has been happening with your family, wish them well in the New Year, and tell them how glad you are that you know them. With current technology, it is easy to personalize it by adding a family photo to

the letter. You might also use one of your child's drawings to write the letter on.

6. You could send a holiday postcard instead of an actual card. This saves you on time and postage. A clever and unusual postcard is to take a family photo and print them in 4 x 6 size. Then address them on the right-hand side and write a note on the left-hand side. Add on postage and you're set.

7. Whatever you decide to send out, don't sit down to write them all out at once. Break up the task and only write a few a night. For example, maybe do one letter of the alphabet each night. You might even carry a small stack with you and when you find yourself with time to spare write out one or two. It's one or two less than you'll have to do later on.

7 THINGS YOU MIGHT NOT REALIZE CAN BE CLUTTER

1. Too many knick knacks, souvenirs, and collections.
2. Walls covered with artwork, photos, and other hanging stuff.
3. Too many pieces of furniture in a room.
4. Papers, magnets, and other stuff stuck to the front and sides of the fridge or kitchen cabinets.
5. An abundance of drinking glasses or plastic ware in kitchen cabinets.
6. Sample sizes of anything, especially makeup, that are not the colors or brands you normally use.
7. Sheet sets for sizes of beds you do not own, well worn sets, mismatched sets, or more sets than you could use in a year.

7 ORGANIZING TIPS FOR A NEW BABY

1. Set up what you can before the baby comes home from the hospital.
2. Designate a space for items you will get that will be used in a few months or years.
3. Keep a few empty bins on hand; this is where you will store all the items as they are used that you want to keep for the future. Be sure to label them clearly.
4. Set up a memory bin now; this is where you will store all the memories as the baby grows.
5. Keep a stash of thank-you notes on hand and write them out the same day you receive a gift to avoid having an overwhelming pile of them to write at one time.
6. Store bulk items, like extra boxes of diapers and wipes on a single shelf in one closet, that way you will be able to shop at home. Replenish from your overflow supply and then restock when you shop. This eliminates the emergency trips to the store or overbuying because you are unsure if you have extra.
7. Make a space in each room for commonly needed items like diapers, wipes, pacifiers, and so on. You can disguise the items in a decorative basket or side table drawer.

7 IDEAS FOR ORGANIZING A PARTY

1. Instead of sending traditional paper invitations, opt for an email version at www.evite.com. The RSVP rate is higher, plus it saves time and money.

2. Label a folder with the event's name and place—all the related notes and lists go in the folder.
3. Create a timeline by starting with the event date and working backwards to plot out what needs to get done.
4. When someone offers help, accept it.
5. Write out the envelopes for thank-you cards in advance of the event so they are ready to go right after the event.
6. If it is a casual affair, go potluck. Prepare the main dish and have everyone bring something.
7. Prepare as much as you can before the day of the event like setting up the chairs and putting out the serving platters.

7 WAYS TO STOP UNWANTED SOLICITATIONS

1. To get off many of the junk mail mailing lists send a signed letter to Direct Marketing Association, Mail Preference Service, PO Box 643, Carmel, NY 15012-0643.
2. Register all your phone numbers, including your cellular phone, with www.donotcall.gov.
3. To stop the preapproved credit card solicitations simply dial the opt out line set up through the Federal Trade Commission at 1-888-567-8688 (1-888-5-OPT-OUT) and request that you be removed. Or you can opt out online at www.OptOutPreScreen.com.
4. When you give your name, address, or phone number to someone request it be kept private and that you not be added to a mailing list.

5. Check the opt out box when typing your information online.
6. When ordering from a catalog ask that your name and mailing address not be sold.
7. Confirm the charity you use does not sell your information before you make a donation.

7 WAYS TO SAY NO GRACEFULLY

1. I'm sorry; that's our family night.
2. Thank you for thinking of me, but I can't.
3. Let me check my calendar and get back to you.
4. Unfortunately I can't; I hope you can find some-one else.
5. I'd love too, but I'm busy that day/night.
6. I've got something personal to attend to that day.
7. Normally I'd say yes, but I'm just overbooked right now.

7 TIPS FOR HOMESCHOOLING PARENTS

1. Create a separate workspace in the home.
2. Post hours that the classroom is open.
3. Color code the subjects.
4. Use a rolling tote in case you decide to work elsewhere.
5. Use a binder with tabs and use a paper clip to mark where you left off.
6. Add a bookshelf to the space and use each shelf for a different category.
7. Make use of the walls by hanging up what you can like maps and charts.

7 WAYS TO PART WITH DEPARTED LOVED ONES' BELONGINGS

1. Give yourself time before attempting to make decisions about their things.
2. Keep in mind that your memories of that person are not in the actual items.
3. Share their belongings with others who knew and loved them. You may not want the teapot collection, but a friend of theirs might.
4. When tempted to hold onto something that is possibly garbage, ask yourself if the person themselves would have kept it.
5. Designate a memory box as a place to store some treasures.
6. Part with the belongings in phases instead of all at once.
7. Make a pillow out of some of the more memorable pieces of clothing.

7 SIGNS OF HOARDING

1. Saving everything, even garbage.
2. Saving things in excessive quantities.
3. Not being able to part with things rationally.
4. Bringing more things home than there is space for.
5. Living in a home that is unsafe, a fire hazard, or cannot be properly cleaned because of the stuff.
6. The stuff affects day-to-day living.
7. The home is so cluttered that people can't come over.

7 TIPS WHEN YOU'VE LEFT CLUTTER CONTROL TO THE LAST MINUTE

1. No more scooping papers into a bag or basket and hiding it away in a closet when people are coming over. Scoop up the piles of paper from the surfaces and place them on your bed. Then you'll at least be forced to put it back before you go to sleep that night.

2. When people pop by unannounced, work on the visible surfaces only. If you have guests arriving, just touch up the surfaces. They are not going to inspect the inside of your closets, so don't worry about them.

3. When people are coming and you are short on space, disguise the clutter. You can stow things under a table and then throw a floor length tablecloth over the table to hide everything.

4. When you were responsible for a project but didn't get it done, just ask for help. If you were supposed to call and remind people about the meeting tomorrow night and you didn't yet, call someone in the group and ask them to help. It is okay to ask for and receive help.

5. When you're hosting a party, contain the party to the living space of your home. There is no need for them to take a full tour including the room(s) where you are keeping the stuff you're going to get to.

6. If you meant to tackle a large project but continually put off getting started and are now almost out of time, just get started. Just moving something breaks the stalemate. You can then make another move and then another. Forget

about the time that has passed. Just get started now.

7. The best idea of all is to just step back, stop worrying, and just be okay with it. Everyone understands—they have clutter in their lives too. Enjoy the moment and forget about the piles.

7 COSTS OF CLUTTER

1. Living in chaos
2. Wasting money
3. Energy drained
4. Lost intimacy
5. Increased housework
6. Stress and stress-related health issues
7. Wasting valuable time

7 EFFECTS OF CLUTTER ON RELATIONSHIPS

1. Arguments and bickering
2. Stolen peace
3. Loss of intimacy
4. Disharmony
5. Dissatisfaction
6. Financial concerns
7. Feeling nervous around all the stuff

7 WAYS FOR A CLUTTERPRONE PERSON AND A NON-CLUTTERPRONE PERSON TO WORK TOGETHER

1. Set reasonable standards.
2. Team up and work together in small blocks of time.
3. Never give up.
4. Take action.
5. Understand what bothers the other person and why.
6. Accept each other, faults and all.
7. Take baby steps and keep restarting if there is a set back.

7 CLUTTERPROOFING ERRORS REVEALED

1. Unrealistic expectations.
2. Going at it alone.
3. Denying the underlying reason(s).
4. Not preparing for the nervousness.
5. Overestimating a project's length.
6. Underestimating a project's length.
7. Marathon clutterproofing sessions.

7 DEFINITIONS OF CLUTTER

1. Things you do not use and love.
2. Things you save with the idea that some day in the future they will be used.
3. Things without homes.
4. Unrelated things mixed in.
5. Too many things in a small space.

6. Anything unfinished.
7. Anything in need of repair.

7 PLACES CLUTTER COMES FROM

1. Abandoned family items.
2. Unwanted gifts.
3. Bought and never used.
4. It's free or on sale.
5. No time to finish, repair, or tidy up.
6. The mail.
7. Too many projects open at once.

7 CLUTTERPROOFING MANTRAS

1. I only keep what I love and use.
2. I can let go of objects from my past because I know the memories live inside me.
3. I get more from having less.
4. How I use my time reflects my priorities and goals.
5. I value my time and energy more than a bunch of stuff.
6. I feel a sense of satisfaction when I can find what I need when I need it.
7. I derive pleasure from a serene environment.

7 SMALL HABITS TO ADD TO YOUR ROUTINE

1. No dishes in the sink or drain board.
2. If you can do it in two minutes or less, do it now.
3. Make the bed every day.

4. Put laundry away as soon as it is done.
5. Take the garbage and recycling out every day.
6. Hang clothes up nightly.
7. Place your keys in the same spot every day.

7 WAYS TO MAINTAIN A CLUTTER-FREE SPACE

1. One new item in, one old item out.
2. If I don't use this in a season, then give it a new home.
3. Before shopping check what you have. Make a list and stick to it.
4. Create par levels. How many extra of each item will you store?
5. Set the timer for eighteen minutes and tidy up every day.
6. Remember the rule: You don't have to put it away, you just can't put it down.
7. Ask yourself "Where will I put this?" and "Do I want to care for this?" before you bring it home.

7 WAYS TO NOT BRING MORE CLUTTER HOME

1. Have the attitude that you value money more than stuff.
2. Do not buy mismatched items—for example, a skirt without its matching shirt because it is on clearance.
3. Ask for consumable gifts like tickets or gift certificates.
4. Remember how many you have at home before you get more of something.

5. Don't buy things just because they are a good price.
6. Make a shopping list prior to going to the store and stick to it.
7. As you attend grand openings and conferences, leave what you don't need behind. Pick up only what you really need, stopping yourself from grabbing it just because it is free.

7 TIPS FOR NEWLYWEDS

1. Open and start to use the wedding gifts that you love. No sense having them sit in boxes.
2. Part with the wedding gifts you don't love or that you could never imagine using. It is okay to do so; it was the thought that counts. If you are uncomfortable doing so, then place them in a large container and if you don't use them by your one year anniversary, part with them then.
3. Tuck a few extra wedding favors and invitations into a memory box. Frame one of the invitations if you like and part with the rest.
4. Work on writing out your thank-you notes a few at a time. Trying to tackle a huge stack at once can be overwhelming.
5. Place your dress and other memorabilia in proper storage and tuck it away.
6. Have your photos developed right away and place them in a photo safe box until you decide what to do with them. You may also get photos from attendees; tuck them in the box as well.
7. Attend to the important papers that you now need. Insurances, wills, advance directives, and

so on. Appoint a new beneficiary on things like mutual funds and make an appointment to handle the other official documents with a lawyer.

7 TIPS TO MERGE HOUSEHOLDS

1. Create a master list of the large items you each own to spot the duplicates and figure out if you can use both or if one has to be given away or sold.
2. Before you part with duplicate items see if you can repurpose them. A medicine cabinet that you do not need in the bathroom might work well in a workshop for small odds and ends.
3. Each of you can choose one item of the other persons that you do not want to have displayed in the living space of the home—say a hula-dancing lamp that does not fit the décor.
4. Each of you can also choose one item that is not up for debate; you are going to keep it no matter what.
5. Tour the space where you will be living together. Discuss what you want to use each room for, and measure the space so you'll know what will and won't fit.
6. Purge and pack. As you pack up your stuff for the move, be ruthless about what you hold onto. Tuck away some memorabilia in a memory box. Overall, you are starting fresh and do not want to carry lots of stuff with you to clutter the space. Instead, leave plenty of room to create new memories.
7. A few weeks after you move in have a chat to discuss how everything is going. Do you each

like where things are placed, is everything convenient, who is responsible for what, is the clutter being kept at bay and so on.

7 ONE-MINUTE ORGANIZING TASKS

1. Put an envelope in your purse for receipts.
2. Put a garbage bag in your car for future use.
3. Velcro a pen by the calendar so one will always be handy.
4. Put a small basket in the laundry room to catch all the items that come out of pockets.
5. Label the tape dispenser and scissors with what room they belong in so they will always be put back in the right place.
6. Weed your medicine cabinet of expired medications.
7. Run a dust cloth over an area.

7 FIVE-MINUTE ORGANIZING TASKS

1. Flip through your Rolodex and purge outdated cards.
2. Make an appointment.
3. Call to see if a store has what you need in stock.
4. Sign children's homework and permission slips.
5. RSVP.
6. Choose your outfit for the morning.
7. Clean out your wallet.

7 EIGHT-MINUTE ORGANIZING TASKS

1. Test all the pens in your pen cup and toss ones that don't work.
2. Return a call.
3. Put in a load of laundry.
4. Toss old food from the refrigerator.
5. Swish the toilet.
6. Clean the kitchen sink.
7. Hang up an outfit.

7 TEN-MINUTE ORGANIZING TASKS

1. Write out a card.
2. Fill a small bag with items you'll donate to charity.
3. Mend an article of clothing.
4. Clean out the junk drawer.
5. Weed the sock drawer and pull out socks without mates.
6. Weed the magazine and catalog pile.
7. Tie up newspapers for recycling.

7 TWENTY-MINUTE ORGANIZING TASKS

1. Iron a few things.
2. Declutter an area.
3. Read something from your "to read" pile.
4. Delete old files off the computer.
5. Care for a pet.
6. Balance your checkbook.
7. Clean out your purse or wallet.

7 WAYS TO HOST A SUCCESSFUL SWAP

1. Send invitations (try online invitations).
2. Make it a party, serve simple refreshments.
3. Create a store like atmosphere and place items by category.
4. Make sure they only bring items they are ready to give up.
5. Have bags on hand for people to carry home swap items.
6. If an item is too large to bring to the swap, bring a photo.
7. Set the guideline of one item for one item.

7 ITEMS THAT MAKE FOR A GREAT SWAP PARTY

1. Books
2. Clothes and accessories
3. Children's toys
4. Recipes and cookbooks
5. Coupons
6. Movies and music CDs
7. Home grown garden vegetables and fruits

7 DONATION IDEAS

1. Clothes: homeless shelters, domestic violence shelters, job training programs, hospitals, disaster relief organizations
2. Toys: children's hospitals, police departments, day care centers, preschools, domestic violence shelters

3. Books and Magazines: school libraries, day care centers, literacy centers, hospitals
4. Furniture: churches, schools
5. Sporting Equipment: scout troops, disabled athletes organizations, camps for sick children
6. Computers: schools, senior citizen facilities
7. Crafting Supplies: day care centers, scouting organizations, homeless shelters, domestic violence shelters

7 CLUTTER-CLEARING STRATEGIES FOR PEOPLE WITH ADD/ADHD

1. Plan the night before.
2. Use a calendar faithfully.
3. Focus on a specific task; try not to multitask.
4. When you put something away, make it easy to remember where you put it.
5. Write everything down—notes from phone conversations, daily task lists, lists of things to buy, and general notes.
6. Talk yourself through the steps as you complete a task and when you put something down tell yourself where it is.
7. Use checklists for tasks, like a list of items needed before you leave for work, and check it before you go.

7 THINGS TO ADD TO A CHILD'S MORNING CHECKLIST

1. Is my backpack packed with everything I need (homework, permission slips, library books, etc.)?

2. Do I have all my homework?
3. Did I grab my lunch box/lunch money?
4. Who will pick me up? When and where? If I'm getting home by myself, do I have my key?
5. Where am I going after school? What will I need?
6. Do my parents know where I am going to be?
7. Do I have the clothes I need for any activity I have (gym, scouts, sports)?

7 WAYS TO CREATIVELY USE YOUR CALENDAR

1. If you are considering returning an item, write the last date you can return it on the calendar so if you decide to return it you do not get stuck with store credit or no return option at all.
2. If you place an order or are expecting a credit, write on the date you are expecting it to remind you to follow up in case you don't get it.
3. Clip papers to the calendar that need action that month, forms to return, or coupons to use.
4. Let's say you have a doctor's appointment and you wrote some questions you wanted to ask next to the appointment time on the calendar. Then you're appointment was changed. On the new date simply write "refer back to xx," the original date where all the information is already written. That way you avoid wasting time having to rewrite.
5. If you need to give something to someone you'll be seeing, write what you need to bring them next to the event where you'll be seeing them on the calendar.

6. Write due dates of library books, homework projects, and other items with deadlines on the calendar.
7. Pencil in the smallest of tasks as well as tasks like reading, organizing, and hobbies.

7 TIPS TO HELP YOU REMEMBER

1. Write it down.
2. Use sticky notes (within reason!) and place them on mirrors, car dashboards, your purse.
3. Keep thoughts together in a spiral notebook.
4. Call your own phone and leave yourself a voice mail message.
5. Record your thoughts on a mini-tape recorder.
6. Email yourself.
7. Set a timer or alarm.

7 CHORES FOR CHILDREN AGE 6 AND YOUNGER

1. Feed pets.
2. Set or clear the table.
3. Sweep.
4. Put away toys.
5. Dust.
6. Sort laundry.
7. Water plants.

7 CHORES FOR CHILDREN AGES 7–12

1. Wash dishes or load the dishwasher.

2. Cook a meal.

3. Wash car.

4. Make beds.

5. Sort and fold laundry.

6. Take out garbage and recycling.

7. Vacuum.

7 CHORES FOR CHILDREN AGES 12+

1. Make lunches.

2. Run errands.

3. Change sheets.

4. Mop.

5. Wash the laundry.

6. Rake leaves.

7. Baby-sit siblings.

7 HOME STAGING IDEAS TO HELP YOUR HOME SELL

1. Have the radio on an FM station or play a relaxing CD.

2. Stow away all photographs of family and friends. They will remind a potential buyer that this is not their home and it makes it difficult for them to imagine living there.

3. Rent storage or move before showing so the home looks more spacious.

4. Keep all the lights on no matter what time of day it is, this will make the home appear larger and more inviting.

5. Bake bread or cookies or simmer a cinnamon stick on the stove for a warm and inviting scent.

6. Post a sign on the front door asking prospective buyers to please take their shoes off.
7. Clear the clutter.

7 CLEANING SHORTCUTS

1. Place wax paper in the bottom of the microwave to catch spills then replace as needed.
2. After using the blender, add dish liquid and water, then blend and rinse.
3. Don't stack dirty dishes. Food residue on the bottom of the dish only makes more work.
4. Use Ziploc bags to marinate meat instead of a dish you'll have to wash.
5. Toss laundry in to wash at night and then switch it to the dryer in the morning.
6. To clean under a dresser, pull out the bottom drawer and clean so you do not have to move the dresser.
7. Wear an apron with pockets so you can carry all the cleaning supplies and have them at hand while cleaning

7 STEPS TO A WORRY-FREE VACATION

1. Turn off appliances and unplug them in every room.
2. Set up automatic timers so your lights will go on and off.
3. Trim the trees back so windows can easily be seen.
4. Lock the door and garage doors.

5. Ask neighbors to be on the look out. Give them a key and your itinerary.
6. Have your lawn mowed while you are away.
7. Ask neighbor to park in your driveway.

7 WAYS TO BABYPROOF THE HOME OFFICE

1. Anchor bookshelves and top-heavy file cabinets to the wall.
2. Bundle cords in a cord control wrapper and check other items at child level.
3. Velcro locks on file cabinets.
4. Give kids a special spot with toys used in the office under your supervision only.
5. Put away the small dangerous things like pins and other items.
6. Cover expensive items like printers.
7. Cover disk drives, outlets, and other enticing openings.

7 WAYS TO PROTECT YOUR PDA, LAPTOP COMPUTER, AND CELL PHONE

1. Back up your information often.
2. Turn on the password option.
3. Pack the item in a generic bag so it is disguised.
4. Use online storage if you want to access your backup from anywhere.
5. Record the serial and model numbers.
6. Always keep it in sight and never check it while traveling.
7. Consider taking out insurance on the item.

7 WAYS TO PROTECT YOUR WALLET AND PERSONAL ORGANIZER

1. Photocopy the contents.
2. Store a spare copy of the items you carry in a safe location.
3. Do not carry your social security card.
4. Make sure your ATM card does not access all accounts.
5. Do not write your pin numbers anywhere near the ATM card.
6. Place your information in it to be returned to you, and offer a reward.
7. Do not include your home address.

7 WAYS TO PROTECT YOUR KEYS

1. Do not label the keys with your address or obvious indications of what they open.
2. Give spare sets to family, trusted friends, and/or neighbors.
3. Place hidden keys around outside of the house and in a magnetic holder on the car.
4. Do not carry your safe-deposit key.
5. Keep membership cards on another ring; that way no one can find out your information by having a clerk look up the card information.
6. Keep a master list of who has a spare key.
7. Designate a single location for important keys such as safe-deposit and disaster-proof boxes.

7 THINGS TO DO IF YOUR IMPORTANT ITEM IS STOLEN

1. File a police report.
2. Check your credit for fraudulent charges for six months.
3. Close accounts.
4. Notify credit agencies.
5. If it is your phone, call it. You never know who might pick up.
6. Send an email to tell everyone in your address book to let them know your cell phone number is no longer valid.
7. Replace all the spare sets of keys.

7 IDEAS IF YOU ARE CLUTTER-PRONE

1. Make better habits.
2. Team up with a non-clutterprone person.
3. Give it a shot, even if you've tried before.
4. Understand the root of the clutter.
5. Prepare to feel somewhat anxious.
6. Set up easy systems first to get and stay motivated.
7. Celebrate every success no matter how small.

7 IDEAS IF YOU LIVE WITH SOMEONE WHO IS CLUTTER-PRONE

1. Never give up; old habits can be changed.
2. Do not give ultimatums; they only make things worse.

3. Try not to set unreasonable standards; perfect is not an option, but progress is.
4. Try not to nag. The clutterprone person is probably already hard enough on themselves.
5. Do not blame. There is usually an underlying cause; they are not doing it on purpose.
6. Never name call. It is not constructive or motivating.
7. Do not deny the situation by calling it "collecting" or offering excuses.

7 BENEFITS TO THE NON-CLUTTERPRONE PERSON

1. A need to care for someone.
2. Sympathy from others.
3. Keeping the other person from becoming fully independent.
4. Enabling the person to clutter.
5. Sense of being needed.
6. Always being right.
7. Avoiding moving forward themselves.

A Note from the Author

Dear Reader,

You can have the simplified life you are looking for! And I just showed you over a thousand ways to make it happen. However, here's the deal: No amount of information will get you there. It's the doing that counts, so set your timer for eighteen minutes and get to work on a space.

Remember that once people get started, they will tell you that the anticipation of beginning was worse than the actual doing, and in fact most actually like it! I challenge you to pick a small area and start to clear the clutter. Then watch what happens. I bet amazing changes start to take place. You'll be happier, feel less stressed, save money, strengthen relationships, reach goals, and so much more!

You can do it! I have the utmost faith in you. No matter if you started before and stopped. This is the time! You now have the tools to conquer clutter for life. Take tiny steps consistently and you can't help but succeed. I wish you the best of luck.

I sincerely hope you have enjoyed reading this book, and I invite you to share your success stories, your most useful variations on the tips, or your biggest clutter challenge. You just may see your name in print. I'd love to hear from you. Please contact my office toll free at 1-866-294-9900 or through my website www.JamieNovak.com.

Happy Decluttering,
Jamie Novak

P.S. Every attempt was made to cover all the areas from emotional attachments to belongings to inexpensive and no-cost solutions. However, if you notice a clutter challenge that was not addressed we'd love to know about it. Tell us what it is and we just may use it in an upcoming book.

Resources

Please note that contact information can change. All contact information was current at the time this book was written. We apologize if such a change has occurred since the time this book was printed. If you'd like to report a change, so we can update future printings please do so at www.JamieNovak.com.

Also please note that the website addresses and other company contact information contained in this book do not necessarily constitute an endorsement of any products or services by the author.

To find printable forms and checklists go to www.JamieNovak.com.

WHERE TO BUY ORGANIZING PRODUCTS

Organizing Solutions
- www.ContainerStore.com
- www.HomeFocusCatalog.com
- www.ShopGetOrganized.com
- www.SolutionsCatalog.com
- www.StacksandStacks.com
- www.Staples.com
- www.LillianVernon.com
- www.QVC.com
- www.HSN.com
- www.Levenger.com
- www.PotteryBarn.com
- www.Organize-Everything.com
- www.HoldEverything.com
- www.LLBean.com
- www.UltOffice.com
- www.Rubbermaid.com
- www.Gemplers.com
- www.TheMut.com
- www.Merillat.com

Desktop File Box
- www.DayTimer.com
- www.Staples.com
- www.Pier1.com
- www.ContainerStore.com
- www.viamotif.com

Collectibles Organization Software
- www.collectify.com

Calendars
- www.DayTimer.com
- www.DayRunner.com
- www.Calendars.com

Closets
- www.CalClosets.com
- www.ClosetFactory.com
- www.ClosetMaid.com
- www.ContainerStore.com
- www.EasyClosets.com
- www.EasyTrack.com
- www.HomeDepot.com
- www.HomeOrg.com
- www.KV.com
- www.PoliForm.com
- www.Rubbermaid.com
- www.Target.com
- www.StudioBecker.com

Entryway and Mudroom Solutions
- www.childcraft.com (bench)
- www.abigwarehouse.com (bench)
- www.target.com (locker)
- www.LLBean.com (locker)

Photograph Solutions
- www.ExposuresOnline.com
- www.CurrentCatalog.com
- www.creativememories.com
- www.ofoto.com

Garage Solutions
- www.Garagetek.com

- www.HyLoft.com
- www.GarageGrids.com
- www.PremierGarage.com

Flooring Solutions
www.Interfaceflor.com

Sliding Shelf Solutions
www.SlidingShelf.com

Miscellaneous
- www.RacorInc.com (Nooks to install into your wall)

NON-CHARITABLE DONATION OPTIONS
- www.Freecycle.org
- www.excessaccess.com
- www.1800gotjunk.com

DONATION LOCATIONS (SOME WILL PICK UP; CALL TO CHECK.)
- The Salvation Army: www.SalvationArmyUSA.org, 1-800-95-TRUCK
- American Red Cross: www.wecollectclothes.com, 1-866-468-7228
- Goodwill: www.goodwill.org, 1-800-664-6577
- AmVets: www.AmVets.org, 1-800-810-7148
- Dress for Success: www.DressForSuccess.org (suits, briefcases, shoes, and other items for a professional image)
- The Glass Slipper Project: www.GlassSlipperProject.org (prom dresses), 1-312-409-4139
- Project Linus: www.ProjectLinus.org (blankets)

- Noah's Wish: www.Noahs-Wish.org (pet care supplies including cages and crates)
- Lions: www.LionsClubs.org, 1-800-74-SIGHT (eyeglasses)
- New Eyes for the Needy: www.NewEyesForTheNeedy.org, 973-376-4903 (glasses and accessories)
- Share the Technology: www.sharetechnology.org (computer equipment)
- St. Jude's Ranch: www.stjudesranch.org, PO Box 985 Boulder City, NV 89005 (used holiday cards)
- Locks of Love: www.LocksOfLove.org, 2925 10th Ave. N. Ste. 102 Lake Worth, FL 33461, 1-888-896-1588 (Donated hair must be at least ten inches in length; look for salons that offer a free haircut with donation)
- Operation Toy Box: 114 White's Lane Louisburg, NC 27549, 1-919-554-1410
- United Way: www.UnitedWay.org
- National Council of Non Profit Associations can help you locate a charity near you www.ncna.org, 202-467-6262
- Learn about other options at www.throwplace.com, 1-202-338-4110 x. 100

RECYCLING AND HAZARDOUS WASTE REMOVAL

- www.EIAE.org
- Earth 911: www.earth911.org (electronics and cell phones)
- Office supply stores (ink cartridges)
- Packing and shipping stores (packing supplies)

- Municipal collection centers (batteries)

MOBILE SHREDDING COMPANIES
- www.shredit.com

CONSIGNMENT AND RESALE SHOPS
- Search "resale shops" at www.yellowpages.com
- www.consignmentshops.com
  *Resale shops give you cash on the spot. Consignment shops pay you a percentage of the selling price once it is sold.

ONLINE STORES
- www.ebay.com
- www.half.com
- www.amazon.com
- www.craigslist.org
- www.quickdrop.com*
- www.foundvalue.com
- www.auctiondrop.com
* Craigs List does not charge a fee for your listing and is the only store on the list that does this.

SWAPPING
- Swapstyle.com (online swapping)

FURTHER READING
- *Don Aslett's Stain-Busters Bible*, Don Aslett
- *Heloise from A to Z*, Heloise
- *Cooking Light: 5 Ingredient, 15 Minute Cookbook*, Oxmoor House

- *Rachael Ray's 30-Minute Get Real Meals*, Rachael Ray
- *Collectibles Price Guide 2005*, Judith Miller, Mark Hill
- Still can't find the product or resource you need? Visit www.JamieNovak.com or call toll free 1-866-294-9900 for more information.

Retention Schedule

(It is recommended to check with your tax professional to see if your needs differ.)

KEEP FOR ONE MONTH
- Credit card receipts
- Sales receipts for minor purchases
- Withdrawal slips
- Deposit slips

1 YEAR
- Paycheck stubs
- Monthly bank statements, credit card, and brokerage account statements
- Social security benefit statements

6 YEARS

- W2s
- 1099s tax return
- Receipts and other back up papers to taxes
- Year-end credit card statements
- Year-end financial statements
- Major purchase receipts (or as long as you own the item)

FOREVER

- Tax returns
- Real estate records
- Anything that shows proof of paying something off
- Wills and trusts

Irreplaceable Documents List

PLACE THESE IN DISASTER-PROOF STORAGE:

- Automobile insurance card(s) and policy(s)
- Certificates of birth or death
- Marriage licenses
- Car registration(s) and title(s)
- Bank account numbers
- Deeds
- Copy of driver's license
- Homeowner's policy
- Life insurance policy
- Investment records
- Mailing list of family and friends
- Insurance cards and polices
- Medical history
- Military records
- Pin numbers

- Residency letter (a letter from the state sent to you at current address to prove you reside there)
- Social security cards
- Tax records
- Will/living will or advance directive or Durable Powers of Attorney for Health Care
- Cemetery plot deeds
- Photo negatives and one wedding and baby photo
- Papers or records that prove ownership (such as real estate deeds, automobile titles, and stock and bond certificates)
- Legal papers (such as divorce decrees and property settlement papers)
- Household inventory

Clutter Clubs

If you are a professional organizer, coach, therapist, author, trainer, consultant, speaker, or clutterprone person who wants to create a community of people looking to change their lives by clearing their clutter, then facilitating a Clutter Club might be right for you. No previous experience is necessary and you do not have to feel comfortable with public speaking. The Clutter Club is a fantastic, fully-customizable way to connect with potential clients while creating a supportive community. If you'd like to offer such a program but do not want to start from scratch, consider using the Clutter Club template with this book as your club resource. Contact the author to discuss how simple it would be to start a Clutter Club near you.

Looking for a Clutter Club to join? They are free and open to the public! Clubs meet monthly (some in person and some over the phone) and are great for getting ideas, tips, and motivation! Check out www.JamieNovak.com or call 1-866-294-9900 to locate a Clutter Club near you or for more information.

Index

C

I

J

K

L

M

O

345, 365, 398, 402, 413
retention schedule, 417, 418

S

sensitive issues, 91–94
separation anxiety, 366, 367
shed, 302
shopping, 16, 62, 65, 72, 73, 173, 212, 224, 250, 261, 263, 328, 333, 351
storage, 87, 97–100, 110, 117, 119, 121, 126, 128, 130, 137, 140, 141, 144, 147, 150, 156, 168–170, 174–176, 187, 190, 193, 195, 200, 205, 249, 273, 276–278, 286, 288, 291, 335, 366, 387, 398, 399

W

workshop, 187–191

T

time management, 59–76, 83, 84, 87, 88

V

volunteering, 67